Two Candles of Peace

Dialogues on Peace and Spirituality
on Personal and Global Levels

Dr. K. Sohail

Dr. Kamran Ahmad

Dedication

To the peace lovers all over the world

Two Candles of Peace

Into

The heart of darkness

of

Religious extremism

and

Political violence

Copyright

Published in 2020 by Green Zone Publishing

A division of Dr. Sohail MPC Inc.

213 Byron St. South

Whitby, Ontario Canada L1N 4P7

T. 905- 666-7253, F. 905-666-4397

E-mail: welcome@drsohail.com

Website: www.drsohail.com

Two Candles of Peace

Sohail, K (Khalid), 1952 –

Ahmad, Kamran, 1963 -

ISBN – 978-1-927874-37-0

1. Peace   2. Spirituality   3. Philosophy

Cover Design: Shahid Shafiq

Textual Design: Marcelina Naini

Table of Contents

INTRODUCTION

Kamran (October 15th, 2019)

I am not a letter-writer. I never was. The tradition of dialogue, however, I have valued greatly. From the Greek philosophers to the courtyards of Samarkand to the tea houses of Lahore. And in my own life, from intense discussions with my own professors to, much later, reflections and ruminations with some of my selected students. There is a way that ideas grow in an open and deep dialogue that just does not happen in isolation.

I was recently visiting Islamabad where, at Mehergarh Center, I conducted a session in a training on Countering Militancy. One of the students asked for some sessions, more psychological in nature, in the evenings. He told me that when he was going through a particularly rough patch, someone held his hand and walked with him, guiding him out. A "life-saver" is how he was described. And all this, while living on the other side of the world. Originally from Pakistan, this person, a psychiatrist, had lived in Canada for almost 40 years. I am always intrigued by people who offer their support to others on a voluntary basis. I took his contacts and once back in Canada sent him a message, wanting to connect up.

Little did I know that this person, Dr. Khalid Sohail, had over 30 books to his name, about 300 articles online and in various publications and scores of video programs online. So, here I was, going in completely ignorant. Within a few hours, I got a reply from him, wanting to talk. And after talking for a few minutes, I was invited to a dinner-meeting in a few days' time. Yes, he paid for the dinner as well. He also invited to the restaurant a couple who had been hosting the Family of the Heart group in Toronto.

At the dinner, I became aware of the intellectual, creative force that I had opened myself up to. He seemed to have an in-depth knowledge of any topic that came up over dinner. What was impressive was that there was no pretense, no arrogance, and no sign of an inflated sense of self. No sign of a self, in fact, as the Sufis would talk of it.

"I have stumbled upon a real-life Sufi", I thought. An intellectual, humanist, atheist Sufi! In an Ontario restaurant!

By the end of dinner, he suggested to me to do a project with him. If there was something that I wanted to explore. Amazing generosity. And within a few days, I received his first letter, initiating the dialogue.

The first letter was about three weeks ago. It generated an intense exchange of letters where over the next 22 days we wrote 35 letters to each other. We poured out our experiences, observations, reflections, and our hearts, in an open, deep, creative and honest dialogue. Dr. Sohail suggested that these letters would be of interest and benefit to others who are on similar quests in their lives. And to share them, therefore, in the form of a book. And that is how this book came to be.

This book would be of interest to anyone who has wanted to get to a deeper place of peace within themselves. Anyone who wants to explore the deeper, spiritual dimensions of their lives. Anyone who wants to be an activist to bring about social transformation and peace in the world around them.

While we explore the inner dimensions of a spiritual life, you do not have to believe or not believe in formal religions or even formal spirituality to benefit from the dialogue contained in this book. It is an honest, open, no-holds-barred exploration that goes from very personal to societal to global levels. Covered along the way are brief introductions to life-changing ideas, and to writers, philosophers, sages, scientists and activists who have influenced and inspired us on our paths.

The two candles bring light first into the personal level. This is the level of finding peace, resolution and integration within oneself. The second level has to do with bringing the light of that inner peace into the world around us. This is the level of interfacing with conflicts, injustice and violence on the societal and global levels. The two candles shine their light into the heart of the darkness within and the darkness around.

While appreciating Dr. Khalid Sohail for all the time and energy, for all the attention and insights that he has poured into this intense exchange of letters, I see his initiative and input as setting an example on a much deeper level as well. In some fields of activity, it is very common to have people working together to produce masterpieces. Take the example of the production of a classic movie. This is where the *whole* is much more than the sum of its parts. This kind of synergetic cooperation is not as common in intellectual and literary pursuits. What I see Dr. Sohail doing constantly is inviting, supporting, and creatively pulling together people to encourage the production of collective works of intellect and art. One hopes that this book serves as an example of this kind of mutual support, encouragement and synergy in pursuit of shared quests.

To retain the actual spirit of these letters, no changes were made in their language while compiling them in the form of a book. Thus the linguistic licenses that are common in conversations and informal exchanges were preserved as such.

To all those who want to bring deeper peace to their personal and collective lives!

4

Two Candles of Peace

Letter No. 1

LOVE, PEACE AND WISDOM

September 23, 2019 at 8:39 PM

Dear Kamran,

Let me start with a confession. There was a time I had a lot of anger and resentment and violence and hate in my heart.

It took me a long time to realize that I had absorbed all those feelings from my environment. It took me a long time to become aware that I grew up in a violent culture. It took me a long time to recognize that as children we can ingest prejudice and inhale hate the way we ingest food and inhale air.

As a child I witnessed husbands beating their wives and nobody protecting those women as it was considered a private affair, a domestic matter.

As a teenager I heard people throwing garbage at my friend's doorstep because he was an Ahmedi, a member of a religious minority.

As a young boy I experienced a war and saw bombs thrown in my city and innocent children, men and women dying.

As a young man I heard people killing in the name of a merciful God.

Growing up I experienced and witnessed domestic and social, political and religious violence, hate and war. Growing up in my conservative, religious and traditional culture I witnessed a lot of human suffering.

It took me a long time to transform hate into love, violence into peace, war into harmony, suffering into healing.

Over the years I grew older and hopefully wiser. I learnt to value and cherish love and peace and wisdom.

I gradually became a peace-loving person.

That is my biggest accomplishment, by biggest achievement and my biggest pride in life. That transformation helped me create a big circle of female and male friends from different classes and genders, races and religions, professions and social backgrounds. Afsheen and you are the most recent additions to that circle of friends, my family of the heart.

If you wish we can exchange a series of letters and reflect on our past and share our journeys and our stories, our dilemmas and dreams, our struggles and successes in life. Our letters might inspire others to reflect on their lives. Socrates said... an unexamined life is not worth living.

What do you think?

I am also curious about your life, your journey, your growth and evolution.

What inspired you to become a peace activist?

Peacefully yours,

Sohail

Letter No. 2

MY GRAIL QUEST

September 24, 2019 at 1:27 PM

Dear Dr. Khalid Sohail,

Here it goes...

It is the age-old, Grail question that I ask of my country: *"What ails thee?"* The answers, I look for within as well, me being part of the whole (as in a hologram, where every part carries a picture of the whole). The core issue I can find is "religiosity", though I know full well that there are no single causes to anything in human systems. But some of the other core issues I find, a general lack of ethics, repressions of sexuality and the feminine, fear of diversity and complexity, etc., are all either closely related to or centrally rooted in our form of religion and religiosity as well.

I do not see the extremists as the core problem. I feel they are only a natural byproduct of the general religiosity in the majority. I want to keep my focus on the majority. I see them drifting to the right, towards more conservatism. They provide the shelter without which the extremists cannot exist. It is this majority that comes up with the excuses for extremism: lack of education, poverty, lack of speedy justice, etc. They come up with conspiracy theories. Without their cover, the extremists would not be able to do what they did and continue to do.

Even partial answers to "What ails thee?" start begging for answers to the next series of questions, on what can be done to counter these factors. This, both on the individual and the collective levels.

This exploration, however, is not an intellectual or philosophical pursuit for me. As Buddha, Krishnamurti and Rumi concur, when you have a poisonous arrow in your

Two Candles of Peace

shoulder or when your house is burning or when someone slaps you in the face, you don't stop to ask philosophical questions. The pain and the urgency do not allow you to.

The reason this quest is no longer just a philosophical intrigue for me is that... I have blood on my hands. Of many. And it just does not come off.

If we are to work on this together on any level, it's important that you realize what this means to me. I will not talk of just feelings but very concrete experiences and choices I have made in my life that bring me to this intensity and urgency.

In December 1992, in the aftermath of the destruction of the Babri mosque, most of the Hindu temples in Pakistan were damaged. In addition, mobs attacked many Hindu homes as well. In one of these incidents in Baluchistan, a family was locked in their house and the house was set on fire. Along with his family, a small child also burnt to death. There were many deaths. Many. But this one kept me awake at night. The screams of the child. And when I did go to sleep, I would wake up, sweating, as if I was there. Again and again.

A few people in a mob can come down the level of actually burning a child alive. But that no one stepped in to say "a child has no religion. Let's burn the rest but, let's save the child." Anyone trying to stop may have been beaten up as well, but I would have known that we still had humanity left in us. That we were still alive.

And I felt tremendously guilty. Not just survival guilt. But because I felt *I* had failed him. And all the others. I had been studying and experimenting with religions and spirituality for years. And as I finished my fourth degree in the US, I had plans to go for yet another Master's. I felt so ashamed of my life. Of my need to 'understand' the nature of reality. All "mind games", I felt.

Many years later, my first book I dedicated to the screams of this child who we burnt alive, in the name of God.

Two Candles of Peace

The same month, in December 1992, I went to London, to formally break my link to the Sufi order that I had been working very intensely with for three years. I was done with formal religions, structured spirituality and personal gods and goddesses, along with all the spiritual masters and gurus.

Summer of 1993, I finished the coursework of my PhD program and moved from California to Pakistan. And I have never regretted that decision. My friends and teachers thought I was crazy. I had degrees in Physics, Consciousness Studies, Spirituality and Clinical Psychology, which, along with my South Asian accent meant a perfect combination to make it big in Northern California. But the urge to be back in Pakistan, in the middle of it all, was too strong.

Within a year of the Babri mosque riots, I was working with the Human Rights Commission of Pakistan (HRCP). HRCP sent me with a journalist and a lawyer in a small fact-finding mission to write on how those affected by these riots in Sindh were doing now. No one knew what this mission meant to me.

With these intense beginnings, I wish my life, from then on, had been a focused intervention into the heart of religiosity and extremism in Pakistan. But it was not so. I had many distractions and diversions that took me all over. Fighting gender-based violence in Pakistan got me seriously consumed for 9 years. United Nations took about 19 years of my life. UN work, as meaningful as it was, if I had not done it, there were hundreds all over the world lined up to take my place. By comparison, the work on religious tolerance that I could have contributed to, my share of it, just got left undone. As an example, during my HRCP days, I had initiated a group of scholars/activists and the invitation said something to the effect of 'the madrassas and the students coming out of them could be the single most significant factor that could tear our society apart'. This was 3 years before Taliban became active in Afghanistan. My brother-in-law, while going through old papers, found a copy of my invitation and showed it to me. He told me to look at the date, 1993, and asked, "If you knew this all those years ago, what did you do about it?"

While I was not doing much specifically to counter intolerance, I had a feeling to stay close to Pakistan. So, in 2003, when the World Food Program (WFP) of the United Nations asked me to be the Head of their Staff Counseling Unit in Rome (managing Mental Health for 12000 staff, in 80+ countries, all working in extreme environments), I could only stay away from Pakistan for 16 months. I hired counselors for other continents and took special permission to move from Rome to Islamabad, to cover Asia myself. The UN graciously bent its rules to allow me to remain an international staff while still being based in my own country for years. This did mean much less salary and a much lower position. While my family loved Rome, leaving my position did not feel like a sacrifice, because my heart was so connected to the social movement in Pakistan.

Somewhere in the middle of it all, I put all my UN savings into the development of a spiritual retreat center, on the peripheries of Islamabad, naming it Mehergarh. The place I never really activated in what it was meant to be. However, having a 24 room residential facility along with halls etc., and situated in nature, it offered my sisters a perfect place and opportunity to conduct their activist trainings and 'countering extremism' kinds of activities there that I stayed tangentially involved in.

In 2009 I showed up on the larger UN radar and WFP had to ask me to move out of Pakistan, anywhere. I chose Dubai, with 9 daily direct flights coming to Pakistan. My second book, *Tareeqat*, I wrote during the time I was based in Dubai. While I could come every other weekend to Islamabad, along with the vacations and missions to Pakistan, I still only survived 3 years there and resigned in 2012 to return to Pakistan without any job in hand. However, during my notice period, UNHCR (the UN refugee agency) told me that if being in

Pakistan was the only concern for leaving the UN, they could offer me the same contract in Islamabad, again bending UN rules, as long as I could cover Asia for their staff like I had done for WFP. This was hard to say no to, so I ended up taking them up on their offer.

One of the factors behind writing my resignation to the UN in Dubai, to return to Pakistan, was an incident that happened in our Islamabad office while I was there to conduct an all staff retreat. We had a suicide bombing in the office where we lost several colleagues and had many injured, some disabled for life. I knew them all well. We pulled out bodies and sent them to hospitals as fast as we could. I remember, picking up half a leg (which I later found out was of the bomber) so that I could uncover the body underneath. I turned the body over to look at the face to see who it was. The face was so disfigured that I could not recognize him. Later I found out that he was my Iraqi friend, Botan, also visiting from the Dubai office. A few weeks earlier, he had told me in Dubai, as we were both planning our missions to Pakistan, that his mother was so happy that he was no longer in Iraq. She had lost one son to the war and was happy that he was out, safe. He was lying in my lap, coughing blood and breathing his last.

After the quick diffusing with staff and families in Islamabad, I flew to Erbil, Iraq with the body of my Iraqi friend. I arranged for the immediate family not to see the face. It was hard answering questions of his young wife, on when and how to tell the children. When asked, I lied to her that he had died instantaneously, with no pain. The hardest for me was facing his mother, though. By the time the body got there a few days had already passed and when I met her she had not a single tear in her eyes. Just a glazed look. She held my hand and said, 'how could this happen?' And that tore through all my defenses. I did not utter a single word to her, but I knew that it had happened because all of us who saw the Taliban gearing up to do what they did, turned the other way. We did not do our part. We did not do our best. We have the blood of thousands on our hands. Including that of our friends. Including that of her son.

I see myself getting carried away with this letter. More cathartic than anything else right now. But the purpose is also to let you know that while I have a long history of being touched by and feeling intensely about the issue and even paying the price for coming back to Pakistan time and time again, I have not been able to raise myself to meet the challenge the way I know I could/should have.

In Pakistan, I did weekly meditation sessions, monthly lecture series on religious tolerance topics, mini-HRCP initiatives, books etc., but nothing of the level that the challenge demanded. Over the years, I also moved away from doing many seminars and talks and other activities typical of the Non-Governmental Organizations, as I feel what is required is a very deep change in the way we are conceptualizing and visioning the problem. This re-visioning could then inform more realistic and more meaningful strategies that may have a chance to put a dent in what we are up against. Given the magnitude of the problem and the momentum building, backward, anything short of it, just seems like putting Band-Aids on deep, gaping, festering wounds.

As I moved away from the UN, the idea was to settle things in a way that I could finally focus more time and energy on my quest. Two years ago, I thought of doing this while being based in Sri Lanka, where I have a small resort/center on the Southern Coast, in the old colonial town of Galle, about 90 minutes from Colombo. As I moved from there to Canada, primarily for the children, that resort just works as a Bed & Breakfast facility for now, instead of the center that I had imagined it to be.

So, here I am, with diversions that indirectly added to my experience and knowledge base, even though they kept me away from directly following my primary quest. The UN part of the diversion also contributed to providing me with some financial independence, where I do not need to worry about working for money to maintain a simple middle-class existence for the family in Canada. So, I have the time and independence now to focus on the quest that I feel has been my calling.

And I would be very honored if you would join me on this exploration, this journey into the heart of darkness.

Best regards,

Kamran

Letter No. 3

A HUG

September 24, 2019 at 2:28 PM

Dear Kamran,

When you finished reading your letter on the phone, I was so touched that if you were close to me I would have given you an affectionate hug. I need to read your letter more than once to digest, reflect and respond in a meaningful way. This letter is just to share my initial reaction.

When you were reading your letter, I could hear you choking with emotions and your voice cracking with passion. It reflected how much your life long struggle means to you and how significant your calling is for you.

I am touched by your honesty, sincerity and integrity. You have already lived many lives in one life. In the brief encounters I had with you I can see that you have a multifaceted personality. There is a scientist, an artist, a mystic and a reformer all in one in you.

I feel honored to meet you and have an opportunity to have a meaningful dialogue with you. Your letter made me aware of your ideas and ideals, dilemmas and dreams, struggles and successes.

I have a better idea about your past now but I am not fully clear what concrete steps you are planning to take in the next few years to fulfill your dream of reducing religious extremism and increasing peaceful co-existence in Pakistan.

I just wanted to share my initial thoughts while I prepare to re-read, reflect and respond to your letter.

Peacefully yours,

Sohail

Letter No. 4

A RAINBOW OF PEACE

September 24, 2019 at 11:02 PM

Dear Kamran,

Let me start with one of my poems.

PEACE

There is inner peace and there is outer peace

There is emotional peace and there is social peace

There is religious peace and there is political peace

There is local peace and there is global peace

These are all colors of peace

And we need all these colors

To create a rainbow of peace.

Dear Kamran,

Your letter is a goldmine. It has so many personal and philosophical, religious and political dimensions to it. Your passion and your commitment to promoting religious tolerance and peace in Pakistan is remarkable. I have not met very many people in my life with such dedication. I felt sad reading all the painful and traumatic experiences you had to face on this journey. You are a brave man to endure all that suffering and still be alive and loyal to your cause.

Dear Kamran,

Let me make a confession. I am not as idealistic as you are. I am not a social or political activist as I have not gone through the experiences and involvements as you have. So let me share a few highlights of my philosophical, professional and creative journey so that you have a better understanding of my life story.

Dear Kamran,

Now that I am entering the evening of my life, when I reflect on my past, I realize that most of my adult life I have been preoccupied with the following questions:

Why is there so much suffering in the world?

How can we decrease human suffering and increase human happiness?

How can we become fully human?

How can we create a peaceful world together?

My preoccupation with these questions inspired me to become an artist, a humanist and a psychotherapist.

Over the decades I also had an opportunity to read biographies and philosophies of very many creative personalities: scientists and scholars, artists and mystics, poets and philosophers, reformers and revolutionaries and I discovered that they were also preoccupied with the same questions as they all cared for the future of humanity. They all belonged to the same tribe that I call Creative Minority. Over the centuries Creative Minority has been guiding Traditional Majority in the slow, very slow, journey of human evolution. What I learnt from those philosophers I shared in my more than two dozen Urdu and English books. The books that relate to peace and humanism are:

From Islam to Secular Humanism

The Next Stage of Human Evolution

Two Candles of Peace

Prophets of Violence, Prophets of Peace

and

From Holy War to Global Peace

Dear Kamran,

When I graduated from Khyber Medical College Peshawar in 1975, I realized that with my non-traditional thinking and lifestyle it was not safe for me to live in Pakistan. If I stayed there I would have been killed or put in jail or I would have landed in a mental asylum as a suicidal patient, not ending up as a humanist psychotherapist. So I left in 1976, went to Iran and then came to Canada to do my FRCP in Psychiatry. After my graduation, I worked in different psychiatric hospitals and then started my own psychotherapy clinic to develop my Green Zone Philosophy (www.greenzoneliving.ca).

In the last few years, I have embraced social media to promote my message of peace, secularism and humanism.

There was a time I called myself an atheist and used to attack religious dogma and superstitions and blind faith. Gradually my position evolved from anti-religion to pro-peace and I started calling myself a Humanist.

Now I write regular columns in Urdu on HumSub internet magazine and present my interviews on YouTube. I have created a YouTube channel titled WOW (Words of Wisdom) with Dr. Sohail.

Last year Dr. Baland Iqbal, son of the famous Hamayat Ali Shair, and I produced 35 programs titled In Search of Wisdom that are present on YouTube. In those programs, we presented four traditions of human evolution.

Religious Tradition of Iranian philosopher Zarathustra that became popular in the Middle East and gave birth to Judaism, Christianity and Islam.

Spiritual Tradition of Indian philosophers, Buddha and Mahavira.

Scientific Tradition of Greek Philosophers, including Socrates and Hippocrates, Plato and Aristotle. That tradition grew in Europe and North America and gave birth to the scientific traditions of Biology, Psychology, Sociology and Cosmology.

Humanist Tradition of Chinese Philosophers, Confucius and Lao Tzu.

In our 35 episodes, we had 16 episodes of Ancient Philosophers, 7 episodes of Muslim Philosophers including Al Kindi, Al Razi, Al Farabi, Avicenna, Ghazzali and Ibn Rushd. We explored how Muslim extremism of Abul Aala Maududi and Syed Qutb were inspired by the teachings of Ibn Taemia. There were 12 episodes of Modern and Contemporary Philosophers all the way from Marx to Hawking to Harari.

We did these programs in Urdu so that more and more Muslims can understand the evolution of human consciousness.

This year when I went to Islamabad to present a paper in a conference; I was pleasantly surprised to find out that a large number of people read my columns and most of them are young university students. One journalist said, "Dr. Sohail, you do not realize you are an inspiration for our generation". I was overwhelmed by their love and affection, even reverence.

Dear Kamran,

The letter is getting longer than I originally planned. I wanted to give you some idea of how I have been contributing to educate the masses and raise social consciousness in my own humble way.

Creating Family of the Heart is part of the same cause. We promote dialogue so that we can promote social and religious tolerance. We welcome people from all walks of life and followers of different traditions so that we can all learn from each other.

I am so excited that on October 5th at 5 pm you will be our guest and we will all learn from your knowledge, experience and wisdom.

Dear Kamran,

I think that if we keep on having a written dialogue in the form of letters we can share our biographies and philosophies with each other and create a book that will highlight our ideas and ideals. I am optimistic that such a book will inspire others to promote peace and contribute in creating a peaceful world together.

What do you think?

Peacefully yours,

Sohail

Letter No. 5

DIALOGUE WITH OR WITHOUT BOUNDARIES

September 25, 2019 at 12:21 PM

Dear Dr. Sohail,

I am honored and touched by your response letters, all within 24 hours. Thanks for sharing your past and your initiatives. You are a remarkable repository of the kinds of knowledge and experiences that my quest requires and I, therefore, would so much love to have you take it on.

My concern with having an exploration in the form of an intellectual exchange with an understanding to possibly turn it into a book later on: In our first meeting, over dinner, I talked about my policy of strategic *munafiqat* [hypocrisy]. I always told my students that what is of primary importance is to gain more and more clarity on where one stands on core issues in one's life, including religion and spirituality. That is one's inner truth, one's *Haq*, the divine within that we grow deeper into, if we live an introspective life with our eyes open, both outside and in. That, to some extent, would be part of the Sufi *tareeqat* [path]. But I believe in putting boundaries around *Haq*, when it comes to revealing it to others, in words, in our behavior, in our interactions within the societies that we live in. Some of the societies we operate in do not respect one's right to express and to live one's inner truth if it makes them feel uncomfortable or uneasy. I say "do not respect". No, we are talking *mob lynching*. We have lost brilliant students to that. You referred to this lack of space as well. So while one wants to open people up to larger universes, inside and out, one wants them to tread carefully in how and when to reveal what, in their interactions with the world outside.

Of course, you know all this. The reason I bring this up here is that I would love to have this exchange with you more in the way I have inner dialogues and explorations, where the concern is Truth alone, *Haq*, going deeper into issues without any concern for social or legal boundaries to start with. Honest and free creative exploration is what is required here. And creativity, as you well know, does not flow freely within boxes, within the narrow confines of rigid frameworks.

OK, so we write for now and see how we feel about it later.

In your second letter, you asked me about the concrete steps. One of my projects is a book, to expand on the first element/chapter, *Ishq* [love], out of the 7 elements that I wrote about in *Tareeqat* [Sufi path]. That one element got the best response from the youth. They said, 'we all fall in love, have sexual yearnings and have heartbreaks but we also go through tremendous guilt and ambivalence about it all as there is no room in our social and religious upbringing for any of it.' They felt so relieved that this aspect of their lives was finally not only validated but connected to the heart of spirituality and declared essential to the awakening of humanity within us. This book now would be a response to their demands. Also, having Mehergarh there (*mehergarh.org*), and my sisters, Dr. Fouzia Saeed and Maliha Husain, who are very actively involved in the social struggles, I do have an opportunity to initiate all kinds of things in Pakistan. My problem is that I don't want to do more of the same. More of what I have done in the past—seminars and trainings. I want the activities and even the broader strategies to be informed and shaped by a deeper re-visioning of the core issues. So, that is the task, the journey, ahead of me.

As I said, we need to be realistic about the magnitude and momentum of what we are up against. It's not just the issue of religiosity in Pakistan. It's showing up all over. And the Leftist, liberal groups in Western nations are in no position to deal with it for all kinds of reasons. The exaggerated and somewhat misplaced notions of religious sensitivity, political

Two Candles of Peace

correctness and cultural relativism keep them from tackling the threat of extremism in some of the religions, where those religions do not reciprocate this sensitivity given their minimal conception or attitude of *mutual* respect. These notions make more sense when they are two-sided. But these are historical patterns. The goddess cultures, in their softness, disappeared when faced with the monotheistic religions in Europe. Tantra, the goddess and all the pluralism of India got eaten up by the patriarchal and Vedic Brahmanism. Shiv temple at Somnath crumbled at the feet of Ghaznavi. And Dara Shikoh would always die at the hands of Aurangzeb Alamgir.

There are sensitivities and limitations on the one hand and demands of creativity and creative exploration on the other. And therefore my need for carefully creating and protecting the space to open up the kind of dialogue and themes that we may be talking about here.

Let me send this out.

With respect and my best regards!

Kamran

P.S.: Do you go by Dr. Khalid or Dr. Sohail?

Letter No. 6

CHOOSING THE ROAD LESS TRAVELED

September 26, 2019 at 12:18 AM

Dear Kamran,

I do not have a family name. Most friends call me Sohail, some like Khalid. No need of Doctor. Feel free to call me Sohail or Khalid whichever you like.

Let me reassure you that I will not publish our letters until you give your blessing. When we finish the exchange you can read all the letters and edit them the way you feel comfortable. I trust your judgment.

Dear Kamran,

I crossed that line a long time ago where fear used to cross my mind. Now I share my truth with no intention of hurting anyone. Writing more than 200 columns on Hum Sub and engaging in passionate and controversial intellectually stimulating dialogues with followers of all traditions have given me some confidence to articulate my ideas and ideals in a way that they are accepted and respected by the people of the Right as well as the Left. But then I do not have a wife and a number of children. Actually that was one reason not to have a family so that I do not feel restrained by them in sharing my truth.

I am curious to know how did you decide to get married and have children and how did your social position on different topics change from a single man to a family man? I admire people like you who can find a balance between their family, professional and creative lives. I confess that I could not accept that challenge.

I am also curious about the family you grew up in. How did your family of origin affect the choices you made in your life?

I would like our book to be a reflection of our biography as well as our philosophy. Nobody can challenge us about sharing the life experiences we had. We are just adding our unique meanings to them. I believe that when ordinary life experiences are impregnated with meaning they transform into extra-ordinary existential encounters. What do you think of that?

I think for this project we can aim for a book by two peace-loving writers who arrived at the same destination from different paths. Our similarities as well as differences will enrich the dialogue.

I want young people to read our book and get mentally prepared to choose a road less traveled. Our book will make them aware of the hurdles and challenges they will face on that road and prepare them for the obstacles they will face and sacrifices they might have to offer. Reading about your experiences with Religion in Pakistan and my encounters with Humanism in Canada will answer some of the questions of the future generations.

I am looking forward to your next letter.

Peacefully yours,

Sohail

Letter No. 7

PEACE CONSCIOUSNESS

September 26, 2019 at 8:16 AM

Dear Kamran,

This letter was not planned. It just came as a spontaneous outpour of my creative juices. Rather than waiting for your next letter I thought I should share my ideas and ideals with you.

Dear Kamran,

I believe that all children everywhere in the world are exposed to social, religious and cultural conditioning of their families, schools and communities. Their parents and teachers, religious and political leaders and poets and philosophers of their times become their role models and their sources of inspiration.

Let me share three encounters with my father, Abdul Basit, that played a significant role in my life, shaping my peace consciousness.

When I was ten and my only younger sister Amber was five, we were playing in the courtyard and by mistake I pushed her and she fell down. She hurt her chin.

In the evening when we were having dinner Amber complained to my dad and said, "Sohial bhai pushed me, I fell and my chin was bleeding."

My dad said, 'Let us stop eating and I ask Sohail to apologize to Amber."

I froze for a few seconds as it was a blow to my ego, my pride.

I scratched my head feeling embarrassed. I was silent for a few seconds that felt like few hours, days and weeks.

My dad insisted, "We will not eat until Sohail apologizes to Amber."

So I apologized swallowing my pride.

I thought the storm was over. But it was not.

My dad asked Amber, "Do you forgive Sohail"

She said, "Yes."

Dad said now we can resume eating.

That one word "Yes" empowered my sister as a girl and taught me as a boy to respect my younger sister. Respecting my sister helped me respect all women in my life. Now I have so many female friends and there is so much mutual respect between us.

My dad was a wonderful role model as a peace-loving person.

When I was 13, Pakistan had a 17-day war with India. We dug trenches in our street and saw Indian planes bombing Pakistan. M. M. Alam shot 6 Indian planes in 56 seconds and became my hero. So after my F. Sc. exam, I applied for the army. My dad refused to sign the papers telling me that if you go to army you will take an oath that if your commander says 'shoot' you will shoot and kill people. You will become a murderer. I was not happy but I kept quiet.

When I finished my MBBS and became a doctor my dad suggested that I go to army.

'Why now?' I was curious.

He smiled and said, "If you join the army now as a doctor you will save lives, not take lives. You will be a messiah, not a killer."

Dear Kamran,

I wanted to share these incidences to give you an idea of how my dad influenced my thinking about war and peace.

My dad who was an agnostic when young became a peace-loving mystic when he recovered from his illness. People thought he had a nervous breakdown. He believed he had a spiritual breakthrough. His transformation inspired me to write a book *"Mysteries of Mysticism"*. My father was a living example of your book *Tareeqat* as he had absorbed all the seven colors of your spiritual rainbow merging into white light.

First you go towards the light.

Then you are in the light.

Then you are the light.

My dad was a peaceful enlightened person and had developed a capacity of deep love. I was lucky to receive that deep love from him that reflects in my writings now.

Looking forward to your letter and your experiences of the two families, your family of origin and the family you created.

Peacefully yours,

Sohail

Letter No. 8

MARRIAGE, CHILDREN AND NAMING OF THE CHILDREN

September 26, 2019 at 4:42 PM

Dear Dr. Sohail,

Touching recollections of your father! It's the little things we do in our daily interactions that can have such a tremendous impact on the lives of those around us. Especially the children. In addition to who he was, as I get to know him through your eyes, what I really like is the way you talk about him. The respect, the admiration and the love.

As names go, I also did not give my children any family name and they hate that very much now. I wanted them to be their own persons, to have their own individual lives and ideas, free of any family or clan or tradition. That was the activist in me. But we make choices for our children which they may or may not want in their lives. While they appreciated that I shielded them from a lot of the "negative" traditional baggage, this one they do not appreciate. And they remind me of that every opportunity they get.

My grandfather was a Chaudhary and he had huge areas of land on the periphery of the older city of Lahore to his name and lots of people living and working on his lands. But then his lands were reduced to a small part, what later became known as Ahmad Park and later still, reduced to Ahmad Block in Garden Town. And then most of that he sold off also, so, while my father and his two brothers still carried the title of Chaudhary, there were hardly any lands left to be a Chaudhary over. The title loses its meaning really in this case. And on top of that, from what I had seen of *Chaudarahat*, of feeling like you are the owner of people's life and liberty, I wanted no part of it. So, I dropped Chaudhary from my name.

I, however, still wanted to retain the last name: Kamran Ahmad, son of Saeed Ahmad, grandson of Zahoor Ahmad, the owner of Ahmad Park. There was still a sense of pride in that belonging. But honestly, I have never lived in Ahmad Park, or even Lahore for that matter, and did not see my kids living there either. So, for my kids, I decided to drop Ahmad as well.

And then there was the issue of local names versus names of foreign invaders. While today we talk of WE Muslims, ruling the subcontinent for many centuries, it was not really a Muslim rule. It was the rule of the Afghans and the Persians and the Arabs. That is why Ibrahim Lodhi was fighting with Babar and Sher Shah Suri with Humayun etc. And for the most part they kept us, the Indian Muslims, very separate from the ruling elite. Iqbal, responding to the need to raise the Muslim sense of self, told us that *our* forefathers had ruled the subcontinent for centuries and fought "great" battles and "valiantly" destroyed many temples like the one at Somnath. OK, so these are more intellectual perspectives, but I felt very strongly that we needed to separate ourselves from all the invaders who did not have roots in this soil and needed to reconnect with our ancient roots in the Indus Valley and Mehergarh cultures. So, my house that I built on the periphery of Islamabad, that I was going to develop further into a spiritual retreat center, I named Mehergarh. I also liked the meaning of the name, "a place of love". And when I had kids, my wife and I named our son Mehr Sagar and then our daughter Mehr Malhaar. Sagar [ocean] and Malhaar [rain] are not Arabic or Persian names and therefore more local, we felt. And then adding Mehr behind made them connected to our home and to Mehergarh and to the soil. We create all kinds of meanings behind these things, I smilingly reflect on it as I write this now.

So, *Tareeqat* I dedicated to them in the following words:

Two Candles of Peace

To the spirit of Love and Compassion, ever flowing in our midst

In every drop of rain, descending upon us from heavens

In every ocean wave, arising from the depths of our hearts

To Mehr Sagar and Mehr Malhaar

Really cool, I thought. But the point is, *they hate* their names! More because we also broke the tradition where the name you call a person by comes first, followed by the second name which is the family name. Why we should follow that tradition, we thought. In Australia, the first name is called the Christian name. In England women had the father's family name before marriage and changed it to the husband's family name after marriage. In India women just had one name. Later when required to fill forms, they would often add Begum or Bibi as they really had no last names. Anyway, we did not need to follow any arbitrary tradition in naming our children and wanted to break all traditions. Little did we know that we would need to answer to our children many years later on why we were doing our social revolutions using them and their names.

But upon more reflection, I realize that whether we think about it consciously or not, we do end up making choices for our children that they end up having to live with, sometimes gratefully and sometimes having to undo these choices. So, I had a friend who had religious parents and he hated religion and the fact that they required him to go to the mosque to read the Quran, even though the *maulvi* [religious cleric] there was abusive towards the children, and not just physically. He always hated his parents for not being able to see through that and having blind faith to leave their child unattended in that kind of an environment. And then I have a dear leftist friend whose son was recently angrily discussing with me why his father could not have trained him in the predominant religious tradition of the land and let him choose whether he wanted to follow a different philosophy or to go with the flow with the majority of the people around him.

The fact is, whether we embrace it or react to it, we all do have programming on such a deep level from our earliest childhood on. All kinds of conscious choices on the part of our parents and a plethora of circumstances that were just the givens. I always laugh when some of my more 'new age' friends say, 'we are all human, we are all the same, we are all equal'. While on a very deep level that may be true, we cannot close our eyes to how tremendously different our childhoods, our upbringing and our life experiences and exposures are.

What was important for me was to realize to what deep levels I was a product of the particular time and space, the family and traditions that I was born into, whether I embraced them or reacted to them. The awakening for me was to realize that no matter how deep I go, there is more inherited stuff that keeps coming out. That, ultimately, we may not be able to step completely out of, to stand apart from, all of our programming and see the reality of the world around us and the Truth, completely independent of it. What would reality look like independent of personal human knowledge or experiences and even beyond that, our biological limitations? What remains important for me in my life is to be aware of my programming. Some that I can see and some that I cannot. And to try to be conscious of more and more of it. Then only does it become a conscious *choice* to hang on to it or to shed it.

More importantly, as much as the children hated their names later on, when we were naming them, it was very easy to reach consensus to break all possible traditions, because both Afsheen and I see things eye to eye as far as most of these traditions go. That gets me to the more flesh-and-blood question you asked, about my marriage.

I do admire people like you who can be fearless and authentic in their beliefs and lifestyle. Only a part of that has to do with having or not having a family and children to take care of. But, yes, that *was* a factor in my case. I often remember now, as I withdraw from any position that I feel strongly about, in view of security, that before I was married and before I had children, I used to be more of a risk-taker. Even in early days of our marriage, as Afsheen and I had similar views, we would often be in demonstrations and protests, with Sagar sitting on my right shoulder. Then came a time when I caught myself thinking twice about going to the thinly-attended vigil held at the Kohsar Market for Salman Taseer, when he was murdered. And I remember being so disappointed with myself for thinking twice about it. What cowardice, I felt. But the fact is, I did not take my child to that vigil. Not all of the "cowardice" is because of having a family, but it certainly makes a difference for me. I know that I am making a choice that affects not just me but could have possible negative consequences for others that I am responsible for.

After coming back to Pakistan in 1993, I jumped straight into social causes. Human Right's Commission of Pakistan, Aman Committee and a new organization/center that had just started the year before, Bedari. Bedari was initiated by my sister, Fouzia, and a few other daring women, on principles that were very different than the usual NGOs (Non-Government Organizations) around. It was not "owned" by a person and had mostly community volunteers carrying most of the workload and managing the place as well. I had background in working in a women's crisis center as a psychologist in California so as soon as I came in, I was offered an opportunity to coordinate the Crisis Center which was one part of Bedari. This was the first primarily *psychologically* focused crisis center in the country. We did have connections with lawyers and shelters and doctors who would all provide voluntary services for the organization. This for me was a volunteer position that I worked in for many years. And the work was highly meaningful, even if it was extremely difficult at times. More later on my motivations in those years perhaps. But I got very consumed in all this work and did not think much of the traditional measures of having a 'successful' adult life: having a well-paying job, a wife and children, and a house of my own. Many years after having returned to Pakistan, with 12 years of US university education, I had none of these things. And I was living a very happy, contented and involved life (credit must go to my parents also for allowing me to get strange degrees and make unusual life choices as far as career goes).

Then came 2001. I realized much later, in hindsight, the connection to having turned 39 and entering the 40th year of my life. Perhaps unconsciously there was that pressure on me also, the approaching 40's. But I remember suddenly having a new questioning from within; of what did I have to show for my life. While many thought that I had done enough, I had set standards for myself that I was not doing well against. The country, that we were going to change completely, was still where it was. Actually it was sliding backward, with increasing momentum. And other than an adjunct faculty position of teaching psychology at the Quaid-i-Azam University and missions for the United Nations that I still insisted on doing as a consultant (resisting the pressure to join them full time, as that would take away my freedom to do all the other things), I did not have a regular paying job and no formal relationship.

As good as my marriage turned out, my wife and children, the fact is that part of the reason I went for the decision at the time was out of an internal panic of 'what do I have to show for my life?' For it cannot be just a chance that in the second half of my 40th year of life, I met my wife for the first time, got engaged, got married and had a child on the way by the time I turned 40!

But that was not all. There was also a deeper, mostly unconscious desire to be in an intimate relationship. My work had me constantly surrounded with women, but when it comes to sexuality in Pakistan, though it does happen outside of marriage, when it does, it is so very complicated, with lots of game playing, heavy-laden with concepts of sin and guilt and obligations and secrecy and an overall sense of sleaziness. Having studied Tantra, having spent all the years in California, I had a hard time not seeing sexuality as something sacred and pure and one of the highest forms of interaction that two people could have. So, the need for a socially accepted intimate relationship, without any of the usual sleaziness was an internal pressure as well.

So the timing, in terms of the readiness from within, was a big factor, but then there is the magic of meeting someone who just 'clicks'. It was more out of love from Afsheen's side and more out of deep admiration and respect from me, at the beginning. I grew to love her on a deeper level only after marriage. What was most important for me, to start with, was that we had the same basic values, the same political orientation and a love for Faiz and Rumi. These things matter, I still feel. In addition to liking their eyes and ears, these things matter. She came from a communist family background where her father, Nadir Qambrani, was a celebrated revolutionary poet from Baluchistan. She was an agnostic, an artist, a poet and loved to sing. I had spent my life studying sciences and philosophy and I think I was unconsciously attracted to her for having all the things I loved but was not as good at. She complemented my strengths, in a Yin-Yang way.

So, the first time I met Afsheen, it was my mother's birthday party where we had about 50 people present and while other people sang as well, she sang Faiz and I was completely mesmerized. You talked about "reverence". Afsheen sang Faiz from the heart with a reverence that I could relate to. In our first meeting, I was telling her what all I did in life and after listening to me for a while she told me how much she appreciated all that I was doing, but also wanted to know why would I be working for the UN. Why was that important to me? That would have been the most attractive detail for most women. So, then I knew for sure!

I have a confession to make. I was never a letter writer. I make my friends very upset on that account. I realize now that I am writing letters like I dance. I love to dance. And I loved dance parties. But right from my student life on, women would get offended as, when I am on a dance floor, I have my eyes closed and I am lost in my own world. Which defeats the purpose of dancing *with* someone.

Let me stop here, for now.

Best regards!

Kamran

Letter No. 9

FRIENDSHIP IS THE CAKE, ROMANCE THE ICING

September 27, 2019 at 7:23 AM

Dear Kamran,

I love the way you write and express yourself. It is like a river flowing smoothly and effortlessly. You sound so genuine, so natural, and so authentic.

Your children's reaction to their names reminded me of my one *not* so pleasant encounter with my dad. As much as I loved him and adored him there was one thing that I was not happy with. After he recovered from his breakdown and became a mystic, one day, when I was in grade nine, he went to school and added Mohammad to my name. It was not the name *per se* that bothered me, it was the fact that he never consulted me. So my secular name Khalid Sohail that I liked very much changed into Mohammad Khalid Sohail that I did not like. I have never accepted it emotionally and I do not use it in my creative writings. You can also see its repercussions after 911. The irony is that an atheist has a religious name and he cannot convince an American Immigration Officer that he is a humanist. These are the ironies of life. Other than this minor disagreement my dad was a caring and loving father.

Dear Kamran,

Even after my dad became a deeply religious person, he was still very open-minded. Maybe it was because he used to be a professor of Mathematics and a teacher of Science. Even when he was a mystic and I was an atheist, we could have passionate but mutually respectful dialogue about our worldviews.

My dad knew I loved poetry and fiction so he encouraged me to have my meetings with my socialist poet uncle, Arif Abdul Mateen. Both brothers had a lot of respect for each other. My uncle used to say to me, "Your father is younger in age but older in wisdom." My uncle dedicated one of his poetry books to my dad.

Dear Kamran,

Since you shared the details of your romance with Afsheen, now let me share a few highlights about my relationships with women. In Canada I dated a number of women from different social and cultural backgrounds. Even though I told them from the very beginning that I did not want to have a family, and they agreed, after 6 months or 6 years they wanted to get married and have children. So we parted.

When I reflect on my last three romantic relationships I can say that

the first one lasted 3 years

the second one lasted 6 years

and the third one lasted 14 years.

Bette Davis was the last one. We were friends for 25 years and then I suggested that we become sweethearts and she moved from Newfoundland to Ontario. Bette had adopted a 2-week old baby from Romania named Adriana. When I met Adriana she was twelve and became like my daughter. She calls me her friendly father. Two years ago when Bette and I separated we had a special meeting and I asked Adriana who she wanted to live with? She spontaneously looked at me and said, "I want to live with you." Bette had no objection.

So for the last two years, we live in a 3 bedroom condominium in Whitby. I have the first room, Adriana has the second room and the third room is for the guests.

Two Candles of Peace

Dear Kamran,

I consider it as one of my proud life-long accomplishments that Bette and I separated respectfully, gracefully and peacefully. In spite of my reassurance, Bette did not believe we could do that. But we did. During our separation, there was no anger, no resentment, and no bitterness. We are still friends and colleagues. Once I told Bette my philosophy of love: *Friendship is the cake, romance is the icing*.

Dear Kamran,

Now let me ask you a question? What is your concept of Love? How do you separate spiritual love from platonic and romantic love?

In your opinion what kind of love Jalal-ud-din Rumi and Shams Tabrez had?

Looking forward to reading your *Philosophy of Love*.

I hope you are enjoying exchanging these Philosophical Love Letters as much as I do.

Peacefully yours,

Sohail

Letter No. 10

ON LOVE AND ROMANCE

September 27, 2019 at 5:42 PM

Dear Dr. Sohail,

What you share is heart-warming. To have the daughter of your partner choosing to stay with you as her father is so precious. But, honestly, more than the contents of your letter, what impresses me, even more, is the openness with which you are able to talk about your relationships. You and I are both rooted in Pakistani culture, both actually having gone to the Edwardes College, Peshawar, even if it was ten years apart, but later, you spent most of your adult life in North America. Again, your long time in Canada alone does not explain your high level of genuineness and courage in sharing intimate personal details with such openness and willingness. But, it must be one factor, even though the openness is primarily about inner courage and character. I, on the other hand, spent most of my life in Pakistan. I find it very difficult to reveal and share personal details when it comes to intimate relationships.

In Pakistan, I feel there is little space and almost no tradition of a blanket permission to share all aspects of one's personal life with everyone. Not that we do not have relationships where we have very deep conversations and reveal our deeper truths and emotions. Those relationships are very much there. But the sense of boundaries and divisions is always there. Some kinds of sharing within some kinds of relationships. The sharing of romantic relationships, from what I have seen in my life and in the lives of my close friends, remained limited to very few family members and very close friends. Sexual exploits, on the other hand, among male friends were always shared more openly, with a wider circle, comparatively speaking. But this was done more as

achievements, as accomplishments. Even more than that...
there was almost a proud feeling of having conquered
something, a show of masculine courage. The image that
spontaneously comes to mind is that of a gorilla standing tall
and pounding his chest with pride. This has a lot to do with our
gender programming (I want to add "unfortunately"
here). Romantic relationships, on the other hand, we shared
only with a select few. And this time, I do want to say openly
that "unfortunately" this heart-opening, falling deeply in love, is
not seen among men as a sign of masculinity and not something
that we feel necessarily proud of, as wonderful, precious, one of
the most valuable experiences of our lives.

When I was writing Tareeqat: *7 Elements of Living
Sufism in Pakistan*, I put Love and Relationships as the first two
elements of lived spirituality in the subcontinent. More than
any other element, more young people have come to talk to me,
to thank me really, for writing about the first element. There is
almost a shame, a guilt associated with falling in love. Like one
is doing something wrong. Something bad. Whereas, this often,
in my experience, and now I speak also from my
psychotherapeutic experience, is the beginning of, the opening
up of true humanity in a person. It is the ability for the heart to
connect, for deeper emotions to flow, that is a necessary
requirement for empathy and compassion. That is what makes
us human. People, especially men, who have not fallen deeply
in love at least once in their lives, I can usually pick out within a
few sessions and I genuinely feel sad about their lives. Not
having access to this softer emotional intensity, there is
something so fundamentally basic missing in their relationships
and their experience of life in general.

As for having the heart open, being able to access deeper
softer emotions, to be able to relate to the pain of others, I am
reminded of an exchange I had with a client. This was a very
straight, married man in the later years of his life, who had
fallen deeply in love for the first time ever, with a woman that
he could not reveal his love to, given who she was. He was

having an emotional outpouring that was interfering with his daily life. He had only openly shared it with one of his friends, who were attending my weekly meditation sessions in Islamabad. The emotions became so debilitating that the friend referred him to me for professional help. In one session, he talked about being parked in a market place in Islamabad and being approached by a small beggar child, the kind that he would always *shoo* away previously. He felt this was the first time that he really looked into the eyes of a beggar child and saw the bleakness of its existence. At that moment a guard came from behind and loudly cursed the child while hitting him in the back with his stick. The child, along with a few others in the parking lot, ran away and disappeared. And this man, sitting in his car, burst out crying. So he quickly drove out, not wanting anyone to see him like that. Looking at me, he gauged that I was not seeing the gravity of what he was sharing. He explained, "You don't know the things I can do, the things I have done, the things I have witnessed without having any emotional reactions. Do you know what it takes to hold someone's nail and if they don't answer you, you tear the nail out. Without having any emotional reaction to it. I cannot have these fucking emotions. I cannot do what I need to...", and he burst out crying again. In my mind, I tried to visualize holding someone's nail and tearing it out. A shiver went up and down my spine.

So, I ask you, Dr. Khalid, to visualize yourself doing it. What if this was a really bad person? What if you even felt the person really deserved it? We may not have any moral or physical issues with it, and yet there is something in us, the ability to empathize with the pain of the other, that holds us back. Most of us. Those who have a heart even slightly open.

A few months ago, I was hearing graphic details from a training participant from Swat about his friend who was slaughtered, head cut off, in the town square. The square eventually got named the 'red square', for that happening regularly there, to anyone who was suspected of being an informant against the Taliban. This participant, with a long beard himself, had tears in his eyes. So did I. And so did most of the other participants, listening to how the mother of his friend, once it was suspected that someone from the family was an informant, was asked to identify which of her sons was closest to her. She thought they would spare that one, but that's the one they took. What does it take to put someone on his knees, hold his head back and cut his neck off with a knife? How blocked does your heart need to be, not to feel any empathic pain, for you to be able to do that?

I know there are many reasons that hearts get blocked. But excessive formal religiosity is certainly one of them. But I also know that falling deeply in love is a powerful way to awaken that heart. To let the blockages melt. No wonder, those who need people to righteously behead others in town squares, do not want people falling in love. Anything that moves the heart threatens them: poetry, music, dance, art, laughter, beauty, intimacy... and love.

Love connects us to our humanity.

I have found that while love within the family can open the heart also, or help to keep it open; nothing does it as powerfully as romantic love. With parents, siblings, even your own children, there is a *given* that there will be 'unconditional' love. One notices the breakdown of it, more than its presence, as we take its presence for granted, as a given. They are also seen, almost as a part of who we are. Or at least very closely connected to one's own identity and self. But opening one's heart to someone completely outside of oneself, in a loving, romantic way, pulls us out of our self-involvement and into a self-less attraction, into a bigger universe. It's not quite self-less but that's the general direction and that is why, I feel it has the power to open us up to connecting with others, and the universe outside, through softer emotions. Love did that to the man who connected with the eyes of the beggar child instead of cursing him away, and cried at him being beaten up. That's the empathic softening of a heart that was otherwise almost completely blocked.

Faiz's poetry is full of this connection, between falling in love and opening up to the pain and suffering of others around, of humanity. Just one example, in his book, "*Naqsh-i-Faryadi*", he has the poem *Raqeeb se* [to the other lover of the beloved] where he describes what falling in love did to him...

Aajizi seekhi, ghareebon ki himayat seekhi

Yaas o Harman ke, dukh dard ke maani seekhe

Zer daston ke masaib ko samajhna seekha

Sard aahon ke, rukh e zard ke maani seekhe...

Learnt humility, learnt to empathize with the poor

Learnt what was meant by hopelessness, unfulfilled desires, pain and grief

Learnt how to understand the hardships of the downtrodden

Learnt the meanings behind cold sighs and pale faces...

~*~

The connection of mysticism to the heart is very close. Especially so, in the case of Sufism, which is known the world over as a Way Through The Heart, through devotion, as opposed to other mystical traditions like the Buddhist or Taoist. Opening and cleaning of the heart and accessing deeper emotions is what it's all about in Sufism. And the romantic love for another, like of Heer for Ranjha, is very much seen to open us up to divine love. It opens the heart to someone outside of one's own limited existence and that is the journey of connecting with the larger universe out there, with devotion and a sense of the sacred. Sometimes in a more pantheistic spirit, which you know all about, in the subcontinent, we don't even make much of a distinction between the beloved and God. Through the eyes of the lover, God, what is divine becomes apparent *in* the material world, in the phenomenal reality, in the beloved.

You told me you read *Tareeqat* already and I have written all about this in there, so I would not go into that here. But remember, I told you about how I used to lie awake after listening to the news of the burning of that Hindu child in December 1992. While I left formal Sufism right after that, because of that, I do know that the intensive Sufi practices in the three years leading up to that, of being consumed in Sufi poetry of Rumi and Hafiz, in Sufi music, in individual and collective *zikr* and *sama* [Sufi practices], all had a lot to do with the opening of my heart so that the news hit me with that life-changing intensity.

In romantic love, while the heart opens up to something outside of one's self and in that I called it "self-less" above, the transformation, I very strongly feel, is within one's own being. It's a change in the state of one's heart, as Rumi would say, of grapes turning into wine, and not about what may or may not happen between two people in the material world. The other person may not even know about it. When I was growing up, in our parts of the world, that was more a norm than the exception. I know this makes no sense to kids these days.

What I find, Dr. Khalid, is that what adds to the opening and transformation of the heart, even more than falling in love, is the pain of separation, of unrequited love. Rumi's most powerful poetry in Diwan-e-Shams came not when he was *with* Shams but when he was *separated* from Shams. Even more than my therapy, I have dealt with these cases while I was teaching at the Quaid-i-Azam University. My students would often talk to me as, one after the other, they would fall in love. They would be hurting, burning in love, and I would be so happy for them. I always knew that this burning is the gift of love. And I wanted them to stay with the burning for a long time, for months, and not to block it out or seek escape in drugs or religion. When the burning gets blocked, like the blocking of any trauma, it turns dangerous and potentially ugly. But to stay with it, and to see it changing a person, melting them into a softer, more emotionally alive version of themselves is like watching magic at play. Powerful!

In those days, with the students, the question of sexuality would often come up also. The male student often, with hormones kicking, asked me about it, feeling guilty and conflicted inside. The Sufi answer, and that of many other mystical traditions, is simple. Mystics are not as worried about the acts as where the acts are coming from, the intention (not *amal* but the *niyat* behind the *amal*). I would often tell them that *if* and only if the girl is ready also, as long as no one is deceiving anyone or pressurizing anyone and no false promises are made, then do what comes naturally to you. And then move on to so much more that is there in the universe. Repressed sexuality can turn ugly, as we have seen in our society. I do see this as one of the key problems with us. Our indirect expression of it, mostly unknowingly and unintentionally, in inappropriate and grotesque forms. I would tell them, on the other hand, if it makes a girl feel uncomfortable or afraid because of the way they are staring at her, even staring at her becomes a sin. I am sure you know Dr. Pervez Hoodbhoy. I was sitting with him once, as he was retiring from the Quaid-i-Azam University, and we were talking about this and he said that this exactly had been his suggestion to his students also when it came to sexuality and the definition of sin.

Through my teaching and psychotherapy experience, through my cousins and friends and through my own living and breathing in Pakistan, I know that we are a nation of hopeless romantics and we all, including myself, struggle with unhealthy expressions of sexuality. The difference is only of degrees. How is that for a generalization, from someone who feels that one should never make generalizations?!

And I never got to marriage. Let me write a short letter sharing with you how I (actually how both Afsheen and I) feel about it, even though we have a very good, friendly and supportive relationship.

So, more in a while! This was long again.

My mind flows all over, so I hope you, dear Dr. Sohail, don't mind following it from this to that to the other.

My deepest regards!

Kamran

Letter No. 11

ROMANTIC AND SPIRITUAL LOVE

September 28, 2019 at 11:32 AM

Dear Kamran,

You ended your last letter with the expression... "my mind flows all over...". That is your free association and that makes your philosophical love letter so genuine, authentic and endearing.

Spending the first half of my life in Pakistan and the second half in Canada I have come to the realization that Pakistani young men and women struggle with their sexuality because we live in a hypocritical society where sex is associated with sin and guilt rather than affection and love.

Because of social segregation and lack of co-education, boys and girls are not allowed to socialize and become friends. Later on, they have arranged marriages with people they do not love so they spend most of their lives in sexless and loveless marriages and become poor role models for their children.

It is my opinion that when those children who grow up in hypocritical families and communities grow up as adults they have a hard time separating lust from love, immature from mature love and unhealthy from healthy love. Many men see women more as sex objects rather than a true friend, sweetheart, spouse and life partner.

Dear Kamran,

I believe that intimate relationships bring out the best and the worst in all of us. Love and hate are two sides of the same coin, reflecting intense emotional attachment. Opposite of love is apathy and indifference, not anger and hate. In unhealthy and immature love we see the dark side of love reflected as insecurity, jealousy, aggression and violence. No wonder we see so many cases of domestic violence all over the world.

In my humble opinion trust, respect and friendship between partners protect them from the dark side of love. Such friendship helps their communication and inspires them to resolve conflicts respectfully, gracefully and peacefully.

In my personal life Bette Davis and I, being close friends, could separate peacefully because we respect each other and trust each other. We want the best for each other.

Dear Kamran,

I was always curious about different spiritual traditions but I never went to spend any time in any Buddhist Monastery or joined any Sufi tradition but you did. I could never become a disciple of any spiritual guru. So I am curious about your experiences with different spiritual traditions. What inspired you to join them and what led you to say goodbye to them? Were you disillusioned or disappointed with them?

Buddha says all human suffering comes from attachment. So to find nirvana you have to detach yourself from your family, from your friends and from your lover.

In some Muslim spiritual traditions love of God becomes a hurdle for the love of the woman.

I have met so many women who told me that their husbands have become Sufis and now ignore their wives and children. There are so many wives and children of Sants, Sadhus, saints and Sufis who feel neglected and unloved. They are full of complaints. Some are even bitter. So in reality their husband's love for God created hate in the hearts of the wives.

How do you think a man can love God and a woman at the same time?

I am asking you because you have been successful in making this impossible possible. How did you do that? You have been able to find a balance between spiritual and romantic love. You did what Buddha could not do. Even Buddha left his wife and child and went to the jungle to find Nirvana. If Buddha was alive today he would be charged with abandoning his family and not fulfilling his family responsibilities.

Even Abraham left his wife and son in the middle of the desert.

On a personal note I knew I could not be faithful to my creative and family lives at the same time so I chose not to have a family and dedicated my life to art and literature and philosophy and psychotherapy. You love Faiz, so I can remind you of Faiz's poem in which he confesses that he could not do justice to both... love and work... so he left both unfinished, incomplete and dissatisfied.

Hum jeetey ji masroof rahey

Kuchh ishq kiya, kuchh kaam kiya,

Kaam ishq kay aarey aata raha

Aur ishq say kaam ulajhta raha

Phir aakhir tung aa kar hum nay

Donon ko adhoora chor diya

[I stayed busy all through my life

Some spent in loving, some in working,

Work kept getting in the way of loving

And love kept getting entangled with work

At last, tired of it all

I left both of them unfinished]

Two Candles of Peace

Love of God or loving and serving humanity is a full time job and love for family is also a full-time job. That is why there were nuns and priests and monks who left their families to dedicate their lives to the Love of God and serving humanity, like Mother Teresa.

So my question from you is that how can any human being do two full time jobs simultaneously?

When I studied the biographies of creative personalities whether poets or philosophers, artists or mystics, scientists or scholars, reformers or revolutionaries who dedicated their lives to serving humanity, their marriages and family lives were utter disasters. I have come to the conclusion that genuine artists and mystics should not get married and should not have families.

Even Nelson Mandela, the most respected revolutionary in the 20th century has confessed in his autobiography that the only regret he had in his life was that he could not be a good father, as he spent quarter of a century in jail and even when he was released from jail he could not be a father to his children because he had become "The Father of the Nation".

Looking forward to reading your spiritual encounters with different spiritual traditions and your insights in balancing romantic love and spiritual love.

Peacefully yours,

Sohail

Letter No. 12

BETWEEN SPIRIT AND FLESH AND MARRIAGE

September 28, 2019 at 6:23 PM

Dear Dr. Sohail,

There is a lifetime of deep reflection and contemplation behind each one of the comments and observations you make in your letter. There is so much there. And my mind has a tendency to go in all directions in response to *one* question! This is so not fair!

Let me narrow it down to a few conflicts that I found to be underlying these struggles. One has to do with the dichotomy of the love of God versus the love of a woman/family. This may represent a much deeper dichotomy of spirit versus flesh/matter.

Then there is the conflict between completely devoting one's life to a creative or social cause versus the more conventional life of marriage, family, 9-5 job, etc. And the question of whether one can do justice to both in one lifetime.

There is so much more in what you write about, but for now, let me focus on these two, starting with the second conflict.

I told you, I married within the last 6 months leading to my 40th birthday. And, as good as my marriage turned out to be, partially out of luck and partially out of design, at the time, it was more an act of desperation, of unconsciously feeling that I did not have much else to show for my life. Having respectful friendly relationships with women, including sexuality, was not something that I was opposed to. But I actually never really wanted to get married and have children. My view was not all that different from yours, interestingly. That, even more than the wife, if you choose to bring *children* into this world, you need to do justice to their requirements and needs in terms of time, stability, money and attention. It was an issue of responsibility and of making *responsible* choices.

For my life, I always wanted to live free to follow my heart, wherever it took me. Growing up I always said I wanted to live like a traveler. And as they say, one should be careful of what one asks for. I ended up traveling so much in my life, living in six countries, over three continents, and traveling to almost sixty, many of them repeatedly. But my adolescent ideal of living my life as a traveler had to do more with the state of mind and way of life, than the actual travels. It's more about the freedom to respond to whatever comes up in one's outside or inside life; with nothing to hold you back. To go wherever the path takes you and then to choose "the road less traveled by" and at times to leave all roads behind and go into the uncharted territory. So, while I was studying Physics at the University of Minnesota, the freedom to decide to take a year off and go traveling. And while traveling, to end up at a monastery in Sri Lanka and on the spot to decide to start living there. Or later in life, to take a volunteer position at Bedari, to run a new kind of a Crisis Program in Pakistan, even if there was no salary attached to it. To some extent, this means relying on the generosity of your parents or others but also the choice to keep one's material needs low.

To my students, I used to say, it's important to feel that kind of freedom during some phase of your life. The earlier the better. I carried that all the way into my 40s. But it was an amazing feeling of not having any obligations. No commitments. No responsibilities. It's never 100%, but came close to it. Being able to respond in any way at any time, allows us to be able to make choices that in my case, I can say, led to life being highly intense and meaningful. And interestingly my life was more useful to others then than it has ever been since.

The dear cousin of my father that I was very close to had this kind of a life as well. He lived in California for nine years, studying anthropology, and then returned to Pakistan and never did a single day of a 9-5 job. He would travel all over the country, contributing to this and that kind of work, tremendously helpful to people and communities. He had no financial commitments. I remember being fascinated with his life. My only concern was that as soon as he came to Pakistan, he did choose to get married and then had a daughter as well and it was his wife who was taking care of the home, financially and otherwise, not knowing when he may or may not stop by from his travels. And that, as you pointed out, does not seem fair.

In relationships, my student days on, I used to say, I do not want someone to be with me because they have signed papers, with God and others witnessing, that require them to be with me, "till death do us part". What an insult, I felt. I want someone to be with me because at that time they would rather be with me than anywhere else in the world. And not a day beyond, if that feeling ever changed. On Sunday, ten years from today, who knows where and with whom I would want to be. How can I schedule my life, "till death do us part?" What a farce!

During the few years before Afsheen, the thought of marriage did start to cross my mind, but I was careful not to get into a relationship with someone who had very different values than mine. That Afsheen wondered why I would also work for the United Nations (UN) when all of my other work was so much more needed in Pakistan and meaningful as such. That mattered. And that she did not look up to a God to give her answers and directions in life. To my students, I always said, it's important to love her for her eyes and smile and walk, but if you are to marry her, pay attention also to her worldview, her aspirations, and her priorities.

And yet, while Afsheen never asked me to make any choices in this or that direction, I found myself taking on the fulltime position with the UN in Rome, that I would never have said yes to a few years earlier. More than Afsheen, it was the news of Sagar coming along that unconsciously changed my priorities.

And that's the heart of that particular conflict that you referred to. I know that I have done well to serve some people in Pakistan in some ways. But I have no doubt that I could have done so much more for Pakistan had I stuck to the decision to not join the UN, in areas that are so critical, in times that were so critical, times that are long gone now. The roads diverged again, after the birth of my son, and this time I took the road that most would have taken. Finally, saying yes to the UN. And so often I wonder of the difference that made. In my life and beyond.

So, yes, it is very important to make our choices carefully and responsibly. There are no right or wrong choices, I feel. We just have to do justice to the inner yearnings and callings. I have known many who gave up on their callings. And I feel sad about that. But as you pointed out as well, I also have known many who went after their passions, responding to their inner callings, to be artists, poets, travelers, while leaving behind wives and children, struggling to fend for themselves and craving for the right to their attention and presence.

There was another highly respected figure in our family. A scholar, who traveled the world, spending time at different libraries, writing brilliant books that everyone was so appreciative of. Only the close family knew how his wife ran a small shop and raised the children.

And then Abdul Nasir, the father of a friend of mine, who joined the *Tablighi Jamaat* and would disappear for 40 days to start with and then much longer later on. He would say Allah would take care of my family. They did not have any financial troubles. But my friend, Saqib, used to hate not having his father around and had a deep distaste for the cause, for Islam, in this case.

So... both Afsheen and I agree with you, that people who have unique callings and who have the courage to follow their deeper yearnings should not get married and start families. And once we do start a family, we need to take our responsibilities towards those we chose to bring along into our lives very seriously.

Beyond that, however, my view that marriage ultimately is an unnatural institution (and therefore involves paperwork and witnesses, to hold us in), that invariably limits us in some unhealthy and unrealistic ways, requires a lot of background before that starts making sense, so I would not get into that here. Khalil Gibran and Osho have some interesting ideas on that, but I leave that for another time.

But here, dear Dr. Sohail, let me transition, using your mention of Faiz. I know when you quoted his verse you are speaking not of him specifically but of the inherent conflict in trying to live two lives in one and trying to do justice to both. But he does serve as a good example. It is true that he *was* absent from the lives of his wife and his two daughters for long times, time done in prisons, time for the Palestinian cause, evenings spent in the tea houses of Lahore and the union meetings of the laborers and the postal workers and on and on. And he may have had many love affairs, physical or not. He remained open to living life intensely, through the heart. And in that, connecting to the pain for the millions, of humanity. His daughters live intense lives, full of commitment, engagement and contribution. And so was the life of Alice Faiz, devoted to human rights struggles. I wonder what my own life would have been like, if not for his poetry to inspire and guide me along the way. And I feel we need to go soft on our judgments of difficult choices that we end up making. Again, this is not about Faiz alone, but true of so many of us. Faiz, as a young man living in India, marrying a British girl, would he have known how the partition of India would change him and the world around him, what would move him so very deeply that he would not be able to not respond? Choices. What did he and his family lose? And what did they gain? And us, along with them?

The reason I said, transition, in relation to Faiz, is the other dichotomy you mentioned, of love for God versus love for a woman and for the world. Was Faiz a spiritual person? He never talked of Allah in his poetry. Almost never. But when the name is mentioned, it shows up in a way that dissolves the whole dichotomy.

Bas naam rahe ga Allah ka, Jo ghaib bhi hai hazer bhi, Jo manzer bhi hai nazir bhi,

Uthey ga Ana-al Haq ka naara, Jo mein bhi hun aur tum bhi ho,

Aur raaj kare gi khalq-e-khuda, Jo mein bhi hoon aur tum bhi ho

[Then, only the name of Allah will remain

He, who is the Invisible, and that which is Present

He, who is all that is Seen, and the Seer as well

The slogan of *I am God* (the Truth) will be heard,

Which is who I am, and who You are

And the masses will establish their rule,

Which is who I am, and who you are.]

This is the God of Ibn al-Arabi that often appears in Bulleh Shah's and Rumi's poetry. This is a god that is acceptable to Einstein and even Richard Dawkins. This is pantheism, an idea that feels true to me.

I grew up hearing *deen ko duniya par muqadam karo* [prioritizing religion over the world]. Spiritual world over the material world. Spirit over flesh. Which is the duality inherent in all the formal dualistic religions. Coming back to Pakistan, I always used to tell people, my goal is to always live a worldly life and I never do *anything* for the "hereafter". More to shock them into thinking about things differently. From transcendent gods to immanence. I would quote Bulleh Shah often, as they mostly respected him, some even revered him, and so saying it in his words made it more acceptable and more relevant and less threatening. Verses like:

Bulleh Shah asmani urdian pharnaen,

Tey jehra khar betha ohnu phariya ei nayen

[Bulleh Shah you seek Him out there, somewhere, flying in the heavens

And all the while you ignore Him sitting right there where your home is]

Even before pantheistic Sufism, it's amazing how strong these traditions were in the subcontinent, of Tantra and of the goddess, where the goddess *was* the body of the world. And where sexuality was not bad but sacred. And where you knew God *through* the material world, *through* your daily interactions with others around.

About the Buddha, however… first, what you mentioned about him unfairly leaving the family behind is well taken, but the detachment business is interesting. While I have a problem with most formalized religions and spiritual traditions, as I wrote to you, I left behind the religion of Buddhism, just like I left behind the Sufi Order. But there is so much wisdom behind many of these traditions. Buddhism turned into a religion, taking on many Sanskrit ideas and got institutionalized with monks and monasteries. But the spirit of the actual practice of *Vipassanna*, of the meditations, is very different. Detachment does not mean to not experience the material world but refers to the craving, the need of the mind to hang on to things. To possess. To own. To marry. To get attached to feelings and experiences and ideas and identities. To not experience them in the moment. In fact, if you are not attached to the memory of an experience and not attached to any expectations of how it could or should be, then you experience it much more intensely in the present moment *as it is*. No depression of the past, no anxiety of the future, just the here and now. Which, as you well know, minus the religious song-and-dance is the new mindfulness craze. But the point is that it does not separate us from the material world but actually brings more intensity to our interactions with it.

Brings to mind, St. Theresa, who would say, "when I eat, I eat; when I pray, I pray". Or the story of the Sufis that you read in *Tareeqat*, where one is criticized by another for enjoying his food too much, instead of practicing poverty, and him replying whether the other was not too attached to his poverty. The point is not to give up the material world but to not be attached to it. So, pretending to leave behind sexuality, as *bad*, but being completely obsessed with it in one's mind, is not leaving it behind at all. This brings to my mind Osho, flaunting his 99 Rolls Royce, once he was independent of the craving. He was making his point, and then rubbing it in, in his provocative style. It's not about not having the woman, or the family or the wonders of the material world, but to include them in the sense of the sacred and to perhaps give up the craving for them.

So, in the Buddhist monastery no one would talk to anyone else, especially during individual meditation times, which was most of the day. The one conversation every day, one-on-one, was with the meditation teacher. So I asked him about sexuality. And his response was very much like that of the Sufi. He said, 'observe closely where the desire originates from. Is it lust or love? That is what makes it healthy or not healthy for you'. So it's not about not having sex. And it's not about not having love in your life. It's about not trying to hang on to it. In some preconceived form. To try to possess it. To be possessed by it. It's all about freedom. And being only *in the moment*. Or that is how I understood it.

So, Dr. Sohail, even after I moved away from the religion of Buddhism, I never moved away from *Vipassanna*, which brings intensity to my engagement with the world and my relationships. And in some ways, my Sufi *zikr* [repetition] of the *kalima* becomes "nothing else exists except for the Divine". How Ibn al-Arabi would explain it perhaps. Or not.

I go on and on and never answered why I moved away from the Sufi Order or my problems with Buddhism and all formal religions for that matter. But later perhaps.

Sorry, my ruminations keep getting longer and longer! And I know how busy and involved you are with so many things in your life. I really appreciate your taking time out to share ideas and experiences with me. This conversation means a lot to me. Thanks!

Best regards!

Kamran

Letter No. 13

SCIENCE AND SPIRITUALITY

September 29, 2019 at 11:05 AM

Dear Kamran,

It is 1:30 am and I am reading, reflecting and responding to your philosophical love letter. I am writing my first draft. When I wake up in the morning I will finalize it and type it to send it to you. I am so glad that you are creatively involved in this literary adventure. I intuitively knew that you had so much more to share with the world than what you shared in your two published books. In those books, you shared your philosophy but not your biography and as a humanist psychotherapist, I believe that biography is as important as philosophy, the creator as important as the creation. In storytelling they say...the more personal the more universal.

Dear Kamran,

I am so impressed how gracefully you answer my difficult and challenging, complex and complicated questions. You have a gift that the world is waiting to hear. I am a humble writer, just a catalyst, to ask you difficult questions so that your creative juices keep on flowing.

I am so glad you met Afsheen that she became your friend, your sweetheart, your wife, your life partner and the mother of your children. Both of you are lucky to find each other and your children are lucky to have such loving parents who are soul mates and wonderful role models. I wish there were more inspiring parents like you in this crazy world.

Your letter reminded me of the story of two monks traveling on the riverside with vows that they will never touch a woman so that they could keep their love for God pure. And then a woman asked the first monk if he would take her across the river as the river was rough. The monk asked her to climb on his back and took her across the river and then came back to continue his spiritual journey. After three days of walking the second monk confronted the first monk and asked why he took the woman on his back. The first monk smiled and said, "I dropped her on the other side of the river but you are still carrying her in your mind for the last three days". Sometimes it is not the occupation; it is the preoccupation that is important.

Dear Kamran,

So far I agree with your ideas and ideals. Now a little bit of challenge to dig deeper into your philosophy as a psychologist and a mystic. It is about your philosophy and philosophy of many spiritual people to live in the *here and now*. Let me share a personal story to highlight my question.

I attended a conference a few years ago in Ottawa in which a psychologist gave a scholarly lecture on the virtues of mindfulness and living in the *here and now*. There was a pin drop silence. After the lecture, when he opened the floor for questions, I raised my mind. I said, "Would you like us always to live in the *here and now*? Does that mean you want us to consciously live like a 2-year-old young child or a 92-year-old woman who have no choice but to live in the *here and now*, the young child because of the immaturity of the mind and the old woman because of dementia.

I asked the psychologist what is the difference between the consciousness of a 42-year-old Sant, Sadhu, Saint and Sufi, a 2-year-old immature child and a 92-year-old demented woman who does not remember after 5 minutes what she had for breakfast. Both the child and the old woman are dependent on other people to be fed and looked after. How are these Sants, Sadhus, Saints and Sufis going to survive and thrive and serve humanity? No wonder Buddhist monks beg every day and, in India, have special seats on trains so that they do not have to pay the fare. Their yellow robes are their tickets. They are at the mercy of the community who offer them welfare.

Dear Kamran,

Let me share my personal choices in life to take this discussion further. When I was sixteen I asked myself an existential question. How can I make my life successful as I was fortunate to have a wonderful gift of life? I chose to have four dreams to make my life meaningful.

1. To become a doctor and a psychiatrist by age 30 and serve as a therapist for 30 years and then retire

2. To write a series of books and create a body of serious literature reflecting my philosophy of life

3. To travel the world and learn from different cultures

   and

4. To have a wide circle of friends from different religious and social backgrounds and create my Family of the Heart

So on my 60th birthday when I reviewed my life I gladly realized that all my dreams had come true.

1. I received my FRCP three weeks before my 30th birthday.

2. I wrote 30 books in Urdu and English in 30 years: collections of poems and stories and essays.

3. I traveled half of the world and visited many cities in the Middle East, USSR, Europe, North America, South Africa and Latin America.

4. I created a Family of the Heart with my creative friends from all over the world.

To be successful, I had to dream and then remain focused and committed. For my creativity, I had to offer all kinds of sacrifices to serve my community and humanity. That is why I say my creations are my love letters to humanity.

I admire scientists and artists and reformers who work hard and are committed to their ideas and ideals and dreams to become fully human and be part of creating a peaceful world together.

I am sure you have heard what Edison said, that 'creativity is 1% inspiration and 99% perspiration.'

I became a humanist and a psychotherapist because I plan my life seriously so that I can read and write and create and serve every day. It is only possible because of my organized life. My clinic is booked for months and I have a one-year waiting list.

Coming back to the psychologist in the seminar he was not a mystic so he could not answer my question. But maybe you, being a psychologist as well as a mystic, can answer the question of how the consciousness of a 42-year Buddhist monk is different than a 2-year-old young child and a 92-year-old woman.

In your mind, how do you create a bridge between science and spirituality? Science asks us to discover laws of nature so that we can predict life events while spirituality is unpredictable, living in the moment, and being like a leaf in the air, flying with the wind, or a flower on the water, flowing with the current of the river.

What do you think of these hundreds of monks living in the caves of the mountains for years and decades meditating and living in the *here and now*?

In my opinion, many Sants, Sadhus, Saints and Sufis who live in the *here and now* are not very responsible in their personal, social, family and community lives. They are dependent of the good wishes of their families and communities.

I hope you do not mind me asking these pointed, in-depth questions as I want to touch the deeper and higher aspects of your personality and philosophy so that you reflect on the deep secrets of life and share your knowledge, experience and wisdom with the rest of the world.

Looking forward to your next philosophical love letter.

Peacefully yours,

Sohail

Letter No. 14

OF SUFIS AND BUDDHISTS

September 29, 2019 at 4:30 PM

Dear Dr. Sohail,

Thanks for continuing to find time for me and for this conversation. Your sharing of the choices you made and how they came true is very inspiring. The importance and power of having dreams, a sense of direction and then the hard and rewarding work of making it happen.

And now for those who live off others...

When I was returning from California to Pakistan, most of my friends from the field of Psychology were not happy. But one of them who were heavily into Sufism, admired Hujwiri [Data Sahib] for having written one of the earliest books on Sufism, congratulated me for the decision to go back to the 'land of the Sufis'. I quietly smiled even then, knowing how little the country deserved that title. But then I returned to Pakistan and started looking for Sufis and, honestly... I could not find any in the Sufi shrines and *khanqahs* of the country. I had my own way of judging them, beyond the beards, turbans and robes that most of them proudly displayed. More spiritual peacocks and religious charlatans than one would have liked to imagine. Quite sad. There were some who were not as 'peacocky' but did not measure up, in my estimation.

Though he would absolutely hate my saying this, from the people that I got to know well, it was Mr. I. A. Rehman that I found to be fitting my criteria of a Sufi more than anyone else. I say that he would hate that, because he believes in humanity and nothing beyond. No gods or goddesses. Lifetime director of the Human Rights Commission of Pakistan and the father of whatever social movement we have in the country. And he often made fun of my spiritual explanations. But in being selfless, in having an open heart, connected to the pain of others around, in living a life of purpose and meaning and devotion to… not God, but humanity, he was more a Sufi than any other I could find in Pakistan at the time. He was, of course, a close friend of Faiz, another person I put in this category. And another who would hate that.

In looking for the Sufis, what you mentioned, Dr. Sohail, of spiritual people living off others, was most troubling. Not contributing to humanity is one thing but then to live *luxuriously* off others and not just that but to actively exploit them in more grotesque ways, was hard to witness.

I got to know the *gaddi nashin* [inheritor of a Sufi tradition/shrine] of one of the larger Sufi orders in the country. He was returning from *Umra* [non-mandatory pilgrimage to Mecca] once and I was going to visit him in his center in Islamabad. The BBC correspondent in Pakistan at the time was a very close friend and so he asked me if he could tag along given that he was doing a piece on the Sufis and wanted some visuals. The "Sufi" was very pleased that the BBC was there to cover his return to the country. The devotees showered him with rose petals. At the door, he took his shoes off and they put their hands on the ground so that his feet did not touch the carpet as he walked over to his throne-like seat. Once he was seated, people started to come to pay their respects and they would all give money, and a person sitting next to him would keep crumbling the bills and putting them in a pile on the side. The pile kept growing. The camera kept rolling. And I kept dying of embarrassment. What is worse is that they felt no shame in that, no awareness of how gross it all looked.

After the bomb blast in the UN office in Islamabad that I mentioned to you, the office had to move to another location. For a few years, they moved to a house close to Jinnah Super Market. I remember coming in from Dubai and seeing the inside of that house for the first time and in shock asking our Admin officer who the house belonged to. Down to the last details, all fixtures, countertops, were of the most expensive quality. Money spent was oozing out of every inch of the house. The headquarters actually also raised that concern about the place, that UN offices should not look so visibly posh. So, before the Admin officer answered, I said: "it has to be either a drug lord or a high-class pimp". Well, it turned out that the house belonged to one of the two brothers, the *gaddi nashins* [inheritors of a Sufi tradition/shrine] of one of the most respected shrines in the Rawalpindi/Islamabad area. So much for Sufism.

If it was money they were taking, that would be one thing. I am reminded of a client of mine, a young beautiful woman, who sought therapy for a trauma that she had been sitting on for years. Her mother had taken her to see a *peer* [Sufi Master] in the area of Kashmir as she was 'depressed'. The *peer* agreed to give her his special blessings and took her to the adjoining room. There she was raped by him, while her mother sat outside waiting, along with many others. She never told the mother what happened. And she was angry mostly at herself for not screaming. These abuse stories are there, connected to most shrines in the country.

But the financial exploitation goes beyond the Sufis, as you rightly pointed out. During the time of the turn of the century, Y2K and all the paranoia around it, my sister and brother-in-law were going on a few weeks of a diving cruise on a Catamaran, along the coastline of Myanmar. The country had just opened up to tourism and there were diving sites and islands untouched by world travelers, which is rare to find these days. While they were both into Scuba diving, I was not, so I would spend my days taking a canoe and paddling off to explore islands close to wherever we would anchor. The point is that these were places untouched by the world outside. On one of these islands, however, there was a huge temple on top of the hill. By the water, I found the place where the locals lived, a typical shanty town, with no electricity or running water, of course. So then I made my way to the top and went into the quiet temple. I closed my eyes and sat for a while. And then the monk (Buddhist) showed up. He was a very lively character. Luckily he knew enough words of English so that we could communicate some. There was an oversized chair in the middle of the hall where he would obviously sit to give his sermons to the villagers. But I noticed something big on the chair, covered up with a beautiful cloth. A religious artifact, I assumed. Following my eyes, he happily removed the cloth and showed me, with pride, a TV and a VCR sitting on the chair. And I saw the wire going into the back, to a big generator. And again, the fact that he was not the least bit embarrassed about it. He could live with luxury, in the middle of nowhere, off the hard work and money of people who barely had enough to cover their bodies. And with no sense of guilt or embarrassment!

None of these examples are unusual. And that is what makes it so bad and worth doing something about.

But, the other thing you brought up, Dr. Sohail, of the *here and now*, is an interesting one. When I mentioned Mindfulness, I called it the new "craze". But, yes, it's old and not necessarily healthy in the way it was, or is, presented. I, personally, see the meditation of trying to be more and more in the *here and now* as an *exercise*. It's easier to compare it to the physical gym, where one would go to lift weights and tone one's muscles. But the point is not to start living inside the gym. The toned muscles and body help us to do physical work and live healthier and better in our physical lives *outside* the gym. *Here and now* meditations build our mental muscle, while we are in meditation. But we cannot live like that *all* the time. A clear example is that there is no *thought* in the *here and now*. Thoughts, language, words strung together to create meaning, cannot but exist in time. Outside of time, in the present moment alone, you can only feel a physical sensation or the presence of an emotion. So, given that alone, not having *any* thoughts, forget communication or planning the future or inventions or science, why would we want that *all* the time? The reason it helps to meditate for a certain time though is that our minds do benefit from the discipline of being able to focus and concentrate better on one thing. Otherwise, there are so many little knots inside, regrets, unexpressed emotions, anger, guilt, embarrassments, painful memories, future worries, financial thoughts, that occupy little bits of our mind and keep us from bringing more of our attention to the task at hand. Not being affected by these, like what we do through therapy, ultimately allows us to think better, to plan better, to love better and to live better. Unless one decides to start living inside the gym, where the exercise becomes your life, which is what the monk does in his orange robes.

To have peace on the mountain top is no feat. The idea is to start being so familiar with that place within ourselves, that we can bring it into the marketplace with us. Otherwise, what's the point?! I totally agree with you.

So, in the monastery, when I started doing the meditations, initially it was mostly the physical discomfort or daily thoughts and worries that would interfere in my attempt to concentrate only on the physical sensations of the breath. And then one would observe where one's mind had wandered off to and gently but firmly bring the mind back to the breath. And as the surface distractions lost their hold, the deeper stuff started to surface. Distractions that had to do with older, deeper emotions and worries. And then one of them in particular one would start surfacing more and more and I would keep detaching, observing and bringing the mind back to the breath. This is over many days and weeks. But then I experienced what happens when a particular kind of feeling finally loses its hold over you, when it dissolves, when you finally detach from it on a deeper level. It would happen in a split second and there was such a tremendous release of energy with each inner knot disappearing. Tremendous joy and relief. So the memory one could still go back to, but the emotional sting attached to it would be gone. And so, slowly the ability to concentrate started to increase as well.

When I finally came out of the monastery, I remember connecting with people *instantaneously* in such intense ways. And it was not just my experience, but they would respond as if they were dear old friends who had known me forever. I could think clearer than I ever had. But then I moved away from regular meditations, and in came the distractions and forgetfulness and dullness... to now, where I told you my mind flows in all directions. Thanks for calling it 'free association' by the way. But free-associating through life, all day long, day after day, is not that good.

So that is how I understand the spirit of Buddhist meditations. The spirit of Buddha's teaching, of regaining control over unconscious painful attachments and conscious cravings, to be able to be where we are more intensely and with more freedom. This is why he did not just stay in the forest but came back to society and launched the most powerful movement against the Brahmanical hierarchical social order that the subcontinent has ever witnessed. And then the message and practices weakened and then they turned into a religion and several centuries later, the Brahmanical tradition was able to completely wipe it off inside India. And if it had not escaped to Burma the teachings of the Buddha, even in the religious form of it, would have been lost forever. But that's a separate story.

The spirit of Sufism, as I understand it, also did not allow one to leave the world. The permission to leave was given by the teacher at particular times when one needed to break through something inside, for specific periods, hardly ever exceeding 40 days. The idea of monasticism was not there in most Sufi Orders.

But here again, is the reason I carry blood on my hands. I talk about the 'true spirit' of Buddhism and Sufism. The real, deeper understanding, the spirit, which of course is the one that *I* hold true. It is this kind of thinking that gives me a sense of righteousness, I find. God-given righteousness! While I have met a few naughty religious people who are knowingly using/abusing religion, almost all of the sincere, pious religious fanatics I have met, all believe deep down that they have the "deeper", the "ultimately true" understanding of religion. And if only others were to see things with this "right" perspective, *theirs*, everything would turn out so good. And in comes righteousness which can justify anything, including the giving and much worse, the taking of lives.

That is why ultimately I feel the whole business of religion is dangerous and unhealthy. It's not helpful to reason out how our understanding of religion, our interpretation, our bringing out the "spirit" behind it is the best way, as in the process we still keep reinforcing the religious institution itself. Adding to its authority. Adding to our dependence. And unconsciously adding to the resulting righteous violence. And the blood on our hands!

On that bleak note…

My best regards!

Kamran

Letter No. 15

INTELLECTUAL BUFFET

September 29, 2019 at 9:37 PM

Dear Kamran,

I am so impressed how you bring the personal and the political, the psychological and the philosophical aspects of life together in your letters.

I am amazed by the diversity of your spiritual experiences and existential encounters in your search for truth.

I am confident that if one day we publish these letters, the readers will enjoy our spiritual feast and an intellectual buffet. It seems you have lived many lives in one life.

Peacefully yours,

Sohail

Letter no. 16

ON 'THE BLOOD ON MY HANDS'

September 30, 2019 at 4:09 PM

My dear Dr. Khalid,

If we publish this exchange, I do not want our readers to miss a single beat. And the phone call you just made to me, to check on me, out of concern and care and love, I feel so grateful for. You operate on intellectual and all other levels, emotional, spiritual, at the same time. It is a pleasure having this intense exchange with you.

You wanted to check on me for having mentioned in passing, again, the blood on my hands. I know it sounds excessive. But I do take that seriously. Remember how I was saying to you that after doing three years of very intensive Sufi practices, when I read about the burning of that Hindu child, I could not sleep at night, because it felt like a failure on my part. And as I say this, I am not delusional (I think) and realize that it can be seen as taking excessive responsibility. But that is what I wish others in Pakistan would feel also. Not to take excessive, but *some* responsibility. I felt there is a lack of collective responsibility, given where we find ourselves today, as a nation.

In the last letter I was agreeing with you on the futility of having spiritual insights and an opening of the heart if after all that one keeps sitting on the mountain top or under the Banyan tree and not want to meaningfully engage in all that is happening around us. Especially when there is so much pain and misery around. Some countries have taken care of the basic needs, physical, emotional, security, of their citizens, so one can sit back comfortably that there are no major gaps around. No fires that *we* need to put out. But then there are some places, like where we come from, where there is so much that is not attended to. Gaping wounds. Literally. Physical, emotional damage, by people, by institutions, that we close our eyes to. And so, one cannot have one's eyes and one's hearts open and not respond to these things. And when one fails to respond to these things, or at least know that one did not do one's best, how does one not feel some guilt around that? How does one not feel like an accessory to these crimes?

Let me choose a non-religious, subtle example first. I remember once while I was teaching psychology at the Quaid-i-Azam University, there was a fight between the Pakhtoon and the Sindhi students. The University administration during Zia's era, in order to depoliticize campuses, had channeled conflicts along provincial lines, and over time given more and more powers to the provincial councils, including responsibilities that completely belonged to the University administration. Like that of allotting rooms to students in hostels. That's another issue, but my students came to class the next day with bandages and stitches and one of them having possibly lost an eye. And now they were sitting together, both sides, in my class. Many of my classes were diverted to the broader definitions and implications of psychology. So, this required some deeper analysis of the conflict between these students who were good friends on a personal level otherwise. One of the reasons that came up was of having to respond when the council leaders hailed them as they depended on these councils to keep their rooms in the hostels. But it was also about honor. How could they not take action when something wrong was happening around them? That was an emotion that they knew I would value. And I did. But upon a brief exploration, it was clear that most had no idea of what the real conflict was. It was a personal fight between the two leaderships and all they were told, as rods and metal pipes were thrown in the middle of the hostel compound (this was the typical practice), was that there was a fight with the Pakhtoon students, "so pick up something to fight with and come!" And they went. One even felt that when there is a fight to be fought, it is not manly not to fight. That launched another discussion on gender and masculinity in the next class. But at the moment, it was about selecting one's fights. In a society where we do have many physical fights breaking out on trivial issues, I would feel so proud if someone said I got my head split open because I said there will be no rape in the police station in my neighborhood. We know that it happens in almost all police stations. It's just an example, but there is so much that we know happens around us that we choose to close our eyes to. I told them you have to fight things but one, there are other ways to fight than being physical, and two, there is so much that is so wrong around us that we have to be careful in selecting what issues are the most unfair, the most painful, that we need to start with.

It really infuriates me when people who are promoting provincial divides or sectarian conflicts, people who are justifying righteous violence turn around and point fingers to others, even USA or India or if no one else, the government, when things go bad. That we do not see how everyone in a system contributes to it and has a responsibility to do something about it.

All the examples that come to mind are too extreme and here we were going to be talking of things spiritual and mystical in nature. But even the little things that we can do to make our system better, we sometimes shy away from.

OK, so a milder example, of not doing enough. Some years ago Pakistan was hit by the worst floods that it had ever seen. Millions were affected. Hundreds of thousands were left without a home or anything to eat. I happened to be working for the biggest Food Aid organization in the world. Of course scores of international staff were flown in and they were working day and night to reach as many people as possible, as fast as possible, but the number of those affected was so unmanageable, with people stuck on rooftops and trees, having lost everything, including family members, and not having eaten for days on top of that. At a time like that, you would think a Pakistani would be so grateful for being in such an organization to be of help, right? And especially because this was the month of Ramzan, or Ramadhan as it's now called. When hearts are softer and everyone is in a giving mood. And when you get many times more *sawab* [reward] in the hereafter for all the good you do here. Well, guess what? While some of the national staff really worked hard, there were those who said we want to leave at 3 pm instead of 5 pm, as we do in Ramzans every year, because "it gets so hard to work in the afternoons; I just want to go home and sleep". One of the senior managers that I would not name, came to me, baffled, and asked if I could talk to them. Because he knew me and my family well, he said, "Please explain to me this kind of religiosity. They see the internationals working here day and night. But most of the nationals don't even want to stay till the 5pm mark, which they are getting paid for, because they cannot work when they are fasting and they cannot give up on the fasting? Even when their people are going through the worst suffering in their history and when they are fortunate to be in a position where they can really make a difference, save lives? What kind of God would be happy with these choices? What kind of religion creates this kind of thinking?" Not wanting him to say that anywhere else, I gently parroted what we always say, "it's not the religion, its people's fault". And instead of religion, we talked about what a manager could do to get as many of the staff members as he could to stay longer. But, honestly, how much apathy should a nation be allowed?

And, as a nation, the next year, come rainy season, we were as unprepared to deal with possible flooding as we had been the year before. No new canals. No deepening or at least cleaning of the existing canals. Or anything else. In a more recent flooding, Angelina Jolie spent a day sitting on the ground with people in the affected areas and listening to their stories, to help bring the attention of the donor countries to give more. In the evening, however, she was given a royal dinner with hundreds present, with food overflowing the tables. With tears and anger mixed, she talked about the conditions of the people she had spent the day with, while looking at all the food present at this wonderful dinner in her honor. She pleaded representatives of other countries and agencies to do more, but also made some strong remarks on the need for Pakistan to do quite a bit more as well. It would have been a slap in the face of any thinking, feeling nation. But it went mostly unnoticed in our case. And as she was leaving the dinner, our Prime Minister gave her his visiting card. No... I am not kidding!

As a nation we have to take our responsibilities more seriously. So, perhaps I say such extreme things also to shock people out of our pleasant collective sleep, but primarily because deep down, I do feel it. If there is broken glass on the ground in your house, it is the responsibility of anyone and everyone in the family to rush to clean it up, before someone gets hurt, right? OK, maybe not the 6-month old. But how many 6-month olds are allowed in a family?

Best regards and once again, my gratitude for your thoughtfulness and caring.

Kamran

Letter No. 17

COLLECTIVE GUILT

September 30, 2019 at 11:34 PM

Dear Kamran,

I am so glad you wrote this letter and shared your ideas and ideals. It gives me an opportunity to share my inner dialogue.

The reason I was reluctant to share my concerns and questions was because I felt you had raw emotions and you were deeply hurt by the traumatic experiences. You were so close physically to the incidents and so intimately to people who lost their lives and limbs. It is like those people who come back from a war and suffer from Post-Traumatic Stress Disorder and keep on having nightmares for the rest of their lives.

I just hope and wish that you heal from those wounds and feel peaceful.

I felt concerned because you felt guilty about what you could not do to prevent those disasters. I think you are too hard on yourself. You are more loving to others and less loving to yourself.

Being a humanist I am against all forms of violence and against all those ideologies, whether religious, economic or nationalistic, that justify violence.

I believe you have contributed towards peace more than most people that I know. You have been lighting a candle of peace in the dark night of fundamentalism, extremism and violence.

You cannot blame yourself because you did not create the dark night or the violent nightmare.

The history of human beings is full of such violent nightmares. If I follow your lead and go on the path of Collective Guilt then I need to feel guilty for so many human tragedies.

Human beings have been killing each other over the centuries all over the world.

Only in the 20th century, in the two World Wars, millions of human beings were killed. Even in 1947 when my parents migrated from India to Pakistan, millions of people were displaced and killed.

If I follow your lead of Collective Guilt then I need to feel guilty as a man because men have been hurting, abusing, raping and killing women for centuries.

If I follow your lead of Collective Guilt then I need to feel guilty as a heterosexual because heterosexuals have been hurting and abusing homosexuals and bisexuals for centuries. Even many holy books are not sympathetic towards them.

If I follow your lead of Collective Guilt then I need to feel guilty as a middle class professional because upper and middle classes have been exploiting members of working-class for centuries. Rich becoming richer and poor becoming poorer.

Dear Kamran,

I hope you get my point. I learnt that lesson from Victor Frankl, the author of *Man's Search for Meaning,* the father of *Logotherapy,* who lost most of his family in concentration camps because they were Jews, but he did not focus on Collective Guilt.

In my opinion, each one of us follows one's conscience and acts accordingly.

In my personal life, I serve my patients as a psychotherapist every day and help them lead peaceful lives and as a humanist writer, I write blogs and books to raise social consciousness and peace awareness. I feel proud of what I do and not feel guilty about what I could not or did not do.

I believe in evolution and believe that human evolution is a slow, very slow process. It might take us a few more centuries to become fully human. You know as an atheist, I do not believe in God, because I cannot believe God could create so many natural disasters (did you know that Insurance Companies call them Acts of God), and if I did, I would ask God why he created so much suffering in this world. Jokingly I say that for centuries human beings have been correcting the mistakes of God.

Dear Kamran,

In the 20th century, after discovering the atomic bomb, for the first time in history, human beings can commit collective suicide and kill the whole of humanity.

In the 21st century, we have a choice. We can choose the road of harmony and peace or the path of violence and war. I hope we choose peace.

So I agree with your ideas and ideals but I disagree with you that we need to focus on Collective Guilt. Your philosophy can make anyone and everyone feel bad and guilty who is not doing enough. When you focus on Collective Guilt it is the revolutionary in you talking not the mystic, nor the psychotherapist.

In my own life, I try to educate the masses so that each man and woman can use their intelligence and conscience and make wise choices. I think actions inspired by love are more precious than inspired by guilt. That is my humble opinion.

After we discuss spirituality we will come back to this topic and share ideas on how human beings can bring peace in their families and communities and how human beings from different cultures can work together to create a peaceful world together.

Dear Kamran,

When I read your letter about your past traumas and your pain I had an emotional rather than an intellectual response. I felt so compassionate that if you were close I would have given you a friendly hug.

Peacefully yours,

Sohail

Letter No. 18

MEN WITH OPEN HEARTS

October 1, 2019 at 2:32 PM

Dear Dr. Sohail,

You have picked up on things so sensitively and have said so much that I feel so grateful for, that I want to reply to this in some detail. So, more on Collective Guilt versus Collective Responsibility later. But first, let me start at the oddest of places.

You mentioned it in the context of making a point, but I was so relieved to read that you were heterosexual. Not that it should matter, either way. But this tells me that your loving care is just that and not possibly mixed with anything else. You have been so generous with me with your time and attention in such a loving way that honestly, the question did cross my mind. But you are also so open about your relationships with all the women, so the thought that maybe he is bi also crossed my mind.

It is sad, to start with, that the mind would wonder whether, behind all the generosity and love, there could be an ulterior motive. But it's worse than that. It's also because the generosity is not with money but with emotional care, in addition to time. And we are not used to men being sensitive and affectionate outside of their interactions with women, outside of sexuality. And that is really sad.

All my life, but especially when I was working with the Crisis Center at Bedari, I was constantly surrounded by women. I was training on gender-based violence, working with women's issues in a relatively sensitive way, and more importantly not responding to women, for the most part, the way they expected a man to behave. I was genuinely so consumed, most of the time, with the intense issues that we

Two Candles of Peace

were dealing with. My sensitivity came more from growing up only with sisters and all of them older to me. And then doing time in California, where emotional talk is common and sexuality is not done in indirect sleazy ways. So, every now and then, those who would feel comfortable enough with me would ask if I was gay. I would say no, but many may not have believed that, for everything else I was doing did not match their picture of what heterosexual men do. And look at me now, doing the same with you. I have certainly lost my ways.

I am really impressed with your ability to connect with people on a heart level. You are so open with your love. I have had the honor of seeing many of the leading social activists in Pakistan up close. Over the years, many of them end up working from a place of anger, resentment and bitterness. And deep down I know that while one can effectively fight for causes from this place, this is not a place that deeper healing flows out of. And that is why it was so good to see you operating on this *healing* level.

There is almost an archetype of the wounded healer. Talking of the crisis center, I have seen it over and over. In addition to the psychologists, I would train groups of volunteers every six months to support women who would come to the center to get support for the crises that they were currently going through. Some of these volunteers had gone through serious traumas themselves. That builds empathy and is very powerful. But only after the personal trauma is worked through. Otherwise, it starts to color their interaction with the woman they are trying to support. Their own issues start to bleed through. They start healing themselves through the other person. And that can really get in the way of the one currently going through the crisis. Without going into details, the point is that a wounded healer, who has gone through the healing within herself, can be a powerful healer for others. But not while she sits with open wounds herself. That has been my experience.

So, I see that gap within myself. If I want to facilitate others to get to a more tolerant place, to a more pluralistic place, I cannot do that unless I am at that place myself. Not being at that place, one can only think intellectually of "intelligent" social interventions. Ideally one needs to be in that place, to hold that place within, and then just being in that place already is an intervention. And from that place what is needed for healing flows more organically, without much intellectual "crafting".

Other than Buddhism and Sufism, one other discipline that is very close to my heart is Taoism. I know you know Lao Tzu and have done a video program about him as well. I used to teach Tai Chi along with the Taoist philosophy. In Tai Chi, the place to reach is where the movement *happens* without you trying to move. To act without acting. Where it's not a mind game, but what needs to be done flows *effortlessly*.

When we talk of people achieving transcendence at the mountain top, the prophets come down with a mission to change things. The mystics, speaking very broadly, may come down also but are not necessarily trying to be social or political figures. Things just change around them *effortlessly*. Many people converted to Islam in the subcontinent around the Sufis. Not necessarily because of their preaching. Most of them did not preach much. They were just *being* and things started to change around them. I am horribly over-simplifying, I know, but just to bring out the principle.

In more recent years, I have noticed myself reacting on levels that surprise me a bit. Thirty years ago when I was living in California, I was still against formal religions but had a genuine heart connection with the mosques of the Black Muslims, with the Fijian Muslims, with strong practicing, preaching Muslims. I could connect with them on a heart level, deeper than the garb they had put on. And from that level, on that level, we could influence each other. Now I sometimes find myself reacting to a 'bearded mullah'. Deep down I know that if all I see is a bearded mullah in him, only the bearded mullah will respond to me. Even though I know there is a father in him, a friend in him, maybe an artist in him that, if I could see, I could have brought out and connected with. I could have connected with the *human* in him. But I lose that opportunity, that possibility, that window, every time I get stuck in his beard and his wife's hijab.

So, I end up reminding myself that while I may still hate particular behaviors, it is not the people that I hate. I remind myself that people are just people; it's not the people who are to be blamed when large groups of them turn ugly and violent, it's some institution behind the people that is bad. What I always hear is the exact opposite of this. That particular institutions are perfect but it's the weakness of people that they were collectively never able to follow them. In actuality, it is the ideologies and institutions that color the meaning that people give to their experiences, observations and interactions that make them lean towards apathy, ugliness or violence. I remind myself that people are just shaped by ideologies and institutions and are themselves never evil.

But coming back to the importance of accessing that place of integration within oneself. If we don't feel it within, we cannot bring it out into the world. Which is what we hear all the time, that working for peace outside starts from feeling that peace within.

So, that is why meeting you is so very refreshing for me. It shows me that it can be done. To sit with an open heart and inspire others to be at that place within themselves. The number of different initiatives for peace and connectedness that you are able to juggle at the same time is impressive and inspiring.

I love Victor Frankl as well. For me, his most important message remained that even in situations where they had absolutely no control over their outer circumstances, there was still something that they could do. Even if it meant not giving up control over how those circumstances were going to affect them. That was a control, he said, 'they could never take away from us'. The same circumstances could make someone closed-hearted, bitter and hateful and they could also make someone connect with others more powerfully, more empathically, with a heart more open than ever before. There is always something that one can do, if one does not give in to apathy and disempowerment. And your life is an amazing example of that. But what is important is the peaceful and healing place that you do it from. Which makes all the difference.

More later, perhaps. But the first point I made, was funny and important to share to start with. I hope you don't mind.

My best regards!

Kamran

Letter No. 19

HOMOSEXUALITY AND HIJABI WOMEN...

October 1, 2019 at 11:27 PM

Dear Kamran,

I am quite amused to read that you wondered whether I am a homosexual or a bisexual, because of my affectionate letters to you. Maybe you did not have very many close male friendships in the past and did not connect with other men the way you are connecting with me. My friendship with you is the latest one in my long series of close male friendships that I feel very proud of. The long list of my affectionate and creative male friends include Rafiq Sultan, Ameer Jaffri, Nauroz Arif, Syed Azeem, Sain Sucha and many more especially Zahir Anwer because we have been exchanging letters for years and decades. Our letters were so affectionate that my ex-girlfriend Ann, before I started dating Bette Davis, used to feel jealous of our friendship. I wonder how your wife Afsheen feels reading our philosophical love letters.

The interesting thing was that when Bette Davis met Zahir she was also as impressed and inspired by his creativity and personality and integrity. She could see why we called each other... our alter-ego.

But that relationship with Zahir, like my relationship with other male friends, was always friendship, never romantic or sexual. I was always heterosexual and never homosexual or bisexual, as I was never attracted to men.

To give you a glimpse of my friendship with Zahir I am sharing a letter he wrote to me before he met me and a poem that I wrote after we met in Toronto.

LETTER FROM ZAHIR ANWAR... SILENT MONOLOGUE

Dear Sohail!

At the outset I am extremely sorry for the delay in writing to you. It is simply unpardonable. I do not wish to cite reasons. There was absolutely none. In fact I could not really find the right mood to communicate, though, off course there were sessions of communication with you, long hours of silent monologue. But that is perhaps no compensation for the one who is on the other side of imagination.

However, I beg your pardon.

Your small and delicate card with a few representative couplets on the front page was a treat to watch. I still watch it and praise it. Your emotional impression about my book really flattered me for days (one reason for delving deep into lethargy). I am just a simple scribble. Camus had been my first love so somehow, I paid my homage to the great soul!

I am touched to think that you are so close to me. I wish I could meet you in my teens when I was like a tornado. I wish to relive those days, once again, with you. Javed knows it full well, that, in Diamonds (a local hotel of Muslim intelligentsia, now so-called intelligentsia) I brought waves of fear among my contemporaries.

Now I am a sane person with an absolutely proper estimation of my own self. I am an ordinary mortal. I write because this is one area where I can express myself. Good or bad, I leave it to the people.

You are among those who have some inborn talents. I am self-made. Hence I consider myself an intruder into the world of Urdu literature.

I do not know if ever I will make it to Canada but there is a 99% chance for me to at least once in my lifetime visit the U.S.A. There stays a man whom I consider a saint, a heaven-sent persona for me. To tell you in a nutshell, I do not allow any single day to pass without memorizing him. He is Peter, my friend, my brother. Pray that I may keep my promise to meet him in his own place.

In near future, there is no chance at all to undertake a luxurious trip. Till then we must communicate through this best art of letter-writing. I hope you agree.

Here, it is not easy to create literature. Drudgery, day in and day out does not allow one to indulge frequently into the luxury of creation. But you or the best of the people write so much.

Sohail, one thing I should say to you clearly, your creative energy is abundant and you use it intelligently. Hence prepare yourself for some greater work.

Soon I will write to you even if you do not write to me. I must pay the penalty.

Always yours,

Zahir Anwar

~*~

Poem

INSPIRATION

You came and you left

You are so far and yet so close

Sometimes I feel as if you never came or never left

When you were here I was silent

Two Candles of Peace

And now that you are gone

I talk to you in my heart and in my mind

You are my alter-ego

With whom I can converse

With my words and my silences

There is so much to share

And there is so little time

The evening of life is approaching

I feel sad when I think

I might never see you again

But I feel joyful

That I have a special connection with you

A creative connection

A connection that transcends time and distance

A connection that brings out the best in both of us

You have been a great inspiration in my life

Sohail

July 2011

For my alter-ego, Zahir Anwar

~*~

Two Candles of Peace

Dear Kamran,

Let me make a confession. After living in Canada for a number of years I realized that Canadian men were generally homophobic. Many of them emotionally froze when I gave them an affectionate hug. They were comfortable shaking hands, drinking beer and discussing baseball and ice hockey. They were generally reluctant to create emotionally close relationships with other men. On the other hand, I found, unlike Pakistani women, Canadian women to be very warm and affectionate. So I decided to have Eastern men and Western women as my close friends. In this way, I could have the best of both worlds.

In the last few years I have also created close friendships with Eastern women.

Dear Kamran,

I also want to share a couple of personal encounters that changed my emotional and social reactions to Hijabi Women that seem to trigger you, like Bearded Men.

In 2018 when I visited Pakistan after 15 years I met many old and new writers in Lahore. One of the new writers was a poet named Ayub Nadeem. He was so impressed by his dialogue with me and Ameer Jaffri that he invited both of us to his college to speak to his students.

So when I entered his classroom I was surprised that all young men were sitting on one said and all the young women were sitting on the other side of the class. I was further surprised, rather shocked, to see that all young ladies were wearing black *burqas* covering them from head to toe, except for their eyes.

After the lecture all young ladies started walking towards me. Then one of them moved forward and whispered something. All I could hear was... "Sir, pick". I leaned forward

Two Candles of Peace

and said, "Would you like me to do something for you?" She said, "Sir, can I take a picture with you?"

I said, "Sure"

When she was taking a picture I wondered what she would see because she was covered with her *burqa*. Then she took out a colorful diary and wanted me to autograph it and write a couplet for her.

After I did that for her all the other women did the same. I smiled to myself thinking that they could have made a photocopy of the first picture and distributed among themselves.

Dear Kamran,

That day I recognized that I was biased against *burqa*-wearing women. Under those *burqas,* there were charming young women who were friendly and funny. I had judged them on their *burqas*. They might have judged me on my beard.

I also met a Hijabi Woman in Toronto who is a wonderful poet. She does not like to shake hands with me because I am *na-mehram* [other than the close relatives that one is not allowed to marry] but likes to take pictures with me for some mysterious reason. One day she even invited me to her house for dinner and dialogue and on another occasion took me out for dinner.

I gradually realized that there was a lively artist behind her Hijab.

I also worked with a Muslim woman in therapy who worked hard to feel comfortable not wearing Hijab. She was so used to wearing Hijab that she felt exposed without it.

Finally I have reached such a stage in my life that Hijabi Women and Bearded Men do not trigger me. Now I know not to judge

..a book by its cover,

...a man by his beard and

...a woman by her *burqa*.

I just found out from my new female Facebook friend in the Middle East that five years ago she used to wear a burqa and five weeks ago she wore a *burqini... burqa* plus bikini.

So there is hope my friend.

Let people reflect on their lives and liberate themselves. All we can do is act as a catalyst. And I hope our book will become a catalyst for many readers.

Peacefully yours,

Sohail

Letter No. 20

ON THE FEMININE WITHIN

October 2, 2019 at 3:09 PM

Dear Dr. Sohail,

I am so honored and touched in reading your exchange with Mr. Zahir Anwar. Two men, connecting as human spirits finding a connection on a deeper human level, beyond all petty homophobic concerns. A role model: men who are comfortable with their masculinity. Men, who are not afraid of, or need not hide, their softer sides. Men who can recognize and acknowledge a soul connection with another, male or female. I hope this also becomes an inspiration for our readers. Again, I am so grateful that you shared this exchange with me.

I left Pakistan when I was still a teenager, and as far as gender goes, I spent some of my formative years, the next 12 years, in the USA. You pointed out the homophobic nature of intimate connections between men and men in North America. So, let me blame the USA for my discomfort. It has become a convenient national characteristic by now... blaming the USA for all our problems. The ones that we cannot pin on India or Israel.

On a more serious note, this repression of the collective feminine, this fear of it, I do see as one of the underlying problems in our collective psyche in Pakistan. And, as opposed to the Western criticism of the country, that all women are suppressed and abused in Pakistan, I find the issue is much more complicated and paradoxical in many ways. No denying that the violence against women, which is present in all societies, is comparatively more intense and more frequent in Pakistan. But our discomfort and our hostility towards women is at least partially for what women represent for us, what they represent for us in our own male psyche. The part of us, as men, that we are so threatened by and so afraid to own.

The feminine runs strong in the ancient traditions of Pakistan, the goddess and Tantra included. It runs strong in our collective psyche to this day. There are many indicators of that. Patriarchal monotheistic religions, on the other hand, are very uncomfortable with emotions, passion, sexuality and the human body. And in trying to adhere to these patriarchal traditions, we men and even women in the society become very fearful of the collective feminine within. I see this very much connected to our tendency to segregate women and where possible to keep them out of the public domain, out of our male sights. The hijab, I see as an extension of this. And the more we try to repress and suppress something that is an integral part of reality and our own psyche, the more grotesquely and powerfully it reappears in the shadow form, as in the excessive use of pornography in the country. So, my goal for myself is yes, to see and connect with the humanity behind the beard and hidden underneath the coverings of the hijab, but I do see the *underlying need* for these coverings as one of the critical deeper issues with our society. Gender is an area where I can easily go off on a tangent.

Coming back to spirituality, it was the mystics who brought love and passion and poetry powerfully back into our lives. That was the part of our collective heritage where the feminine, the Anima, was kept alive and kicking. But that's another long discussion for another day.

Again, my heartfelt gratitude and my best regards for now.

Kamran

Letter No. 21

MYSTIC POETRY

October 2, 2019 at 10:58 PM

Dear Kamran,

Now let me add another dimension to our discussion. It is the dimension of mystic poetry. Let me share a short essay I wrote about Sehdev Kumar, Kabir Das and mystic poetry, that I presented in one of our Family of the Heart seminars. I hope you like it. Here it is:

~*~

Nearly twenty-five years ago, while I was developing a keen interest in mystic poetry, I came across a book titled *The Vision of Kabir.* In that book, Kabir's mystic poetry was translated in English by a mystic philosopher, Sehdev Kumar. In that scholarly book, Sehdev Kumar had not only provided an in-depth analysis of Kabir's vision and the essence of Kabir's philosophy, he had also shared his insights on the psyche of mystic poetry at large. I had no idea that one day I will have the honor of meeting and befriending the translator and philosopher, Sehdev Kumar.

Looking back now I can say that mystic poet Kabir introduced me to mystic philosopher Sehdev Kumar and the philosopher introduced me to the poet and they both introduced me to the magic and the mystery of mystic poetry. Such an introduction inspired me further in the exploration of the rich heritage of mystic poetry in the East as well as the West and my studies of different cultural and spiritual traditions.

Mystic poetry has a unique position in the family of the world literature because it focuses on:

- internal rather than external realities,

- inner rather than outer truths,

- metaphysical rather than physical journeys, and

- spiritual rather than materialistic worlds.

Mystic poets are those enlightened beings who have personal encounters with the spiritual world and have touched the borders of the known with the unknown, the human with the divine, the personal with the cosmic. They share with us that their experiences are intimate encounters with a world which is nameless, formless, timeless and pathless.

When mystic poets express themselves in poetry they are more concerned about sharing their spiritual experiences, mystical encounters and existential truths and less preoccupied with the technique, form and language of their presentation.

Mystic poets see a human being, a human self and a human consciousness as a drop of water and the eternal truth and cosmic consciousness as an ocean.

Kabir says:

"A drop

is merged

into the ocean

that everyone

understands;

but how

the ocean

is contained

in the drop

Two Candles of Peace

that, O my friend

only a rare man

can comprehend."

One of the most abiding symbols in mystic poetry is light. Mystic poets highlight that after traveling in the dark alleys of one's soul and on convoluted paths of the spiritual labyrinth, human beings reach a stage where they discover their inner light.

Kabir says:

"I shall make

my body into

a clay-lamp,

my soul, its wick

and my blood oil

ah, the light

of this lamp

would reveal

the face

of my beloved

to me."

What is most endearing about mystic poetry is the simplicity of language; it reaches out to touch everyone, everywhere. For a mystic nothing is ordinary; everything and everyone is grand and extraordinary. The mystic looks at the most ordinary everyday aspects of life and uses them as metaphors for illumination for the wonder of life. A potter, a weaver, a flute player, a fisherman – for a mystic, all become part of the grand tapestry of life.

As such mystic poetry does not fit in easily into traditional poetry; for the Sants, Sadhus, Saints and Sufis, their verses and poetry are expressions of their exalted vision and being, rather than a labored art.

Sehdev Kumar, a research scholar of the poetry of Kabir, writes: "...Kabir was first and foremost a visionary, his poetry is a mere "by-product of his vision"...Kabir is a *nirgunibhakta*—a lover of the formless and infinite," and as such it should not be judged as poetry. The verses of the saints are of an entirely different genre than those of the poets. From the pen of William Kingland, we read:

"The mystic may not always be a master of language, but it is truth which he endeavours to express that we should do well to seize; and learn also to make proper allowance for the inadequacy of language to express the deepest truths. No one knows better than the greatest master of technique how inadequate are the materials with which he has to work, no one realizes more clearly than the greatest master of language, how little language can express of the living truth with which his innermost nature is on fire."

With his new book, *How's & Why's of An Unexpected Universe*, Sehdev Kumar is carrying the Vision of Kabir further into his own life, and into the lives of all us, as each one of us, in our own way search for what is fulfilling and enlightening for us.

Dear Kamran,

When my dear friend Sehdev Kumar will be back from India next year in summer, I will invite you to meet him. I will try to become a creative bridge between the two mystic scholars and spiritual philosophers.

Now let me ask you one more question. What are your views about two mystics of the 20th century: the famous J. Krishnamurti, a member of the Theosophical Society of India, and the notorious, Osho, Guru Rajneesh who collected 99 Rolls Royces and claimed that he slept with more women than any other man in the history of mankind?

Looking forward to reading your psychological and spiritual insights on the personalities, philosophies and politics of Krishnamurti and Osho.

Peacefully yours,

Sohail

Letter No. 22

FROM SPIRITUAL TROLLING TO TOTALING SPIRITUALITY

October 3, 2019 at 8:58 PM

Dear Dr. Sohail,

I would be honored to meet your friend Sehdev Kumar. From what you quote and the way you talk of him, he seems to 'know' what he is writing about. Extracting meaning out of spiritual poetry is not easy. If it were, the mystic poets may have just written about it themselves. In my first book, I did that with Damodar's Heer. It's hard to do. But I have seen it done well and from what you say, Sehdev Kumar seems to have succeeded.

Most of the mystics wrote poetry instead of writing philosophical or theological books to refer to the truth they found in their mystical experiences. And as you pointed out, it is probably because language, prose, just does not do justice to these experiences. The power of poetry is that it only points to the truth, suggestively, in symbols and metaphors, moving something within us that may open us up to experiencing it for ourselves. It comes out of, not the mind but the heart, and therefore has a much better chance of touching and awakening the heart to the deeper truths. But then there are so many kinds of mystical poetry and it's not fair to pigeonhole it.

We see the range so powerfully in Rumi's poetry. From pure spontaneous expressions of passionate experiences to teaching stories done in poetic form. He started writing poetry only after he turned 40. This was after he met and fell in love with his teacher Shams, as you well know. And I should not say "started *writing*", as he would often not *write* poetry. He would just dance and spontaneously utter these verses and others around him would write them down. The pleasures of encountering a wandering spirit who opened him up to spirituality and then the pain of him disappearing, the burning of separation, and then the union with him once he returned for a while to leave again forever. But Shams never left the second time, for by then Rumi had merged with him enough that Shams could not be taken away from him. Which is why Rumi named his first poetry collection, the Diwan of *Shams*, not his own. He saw it as Shams speaking through him. Becoming one with the Divine and then perhaps seeing the Divine in everyone and in everything. Was he a pantheist? It would seem so. But then why the *Masnavi* [a massive collection, over six volumes, of Sufi poetry, considered by many as the most important of all the Sufi texts ever written]?

In all the volumes of the *Masnavi*, though Rumi still writes in poetry, the purpose seems to be much different. This is where he comes down from the mountain top, having seen, having experienced, having *been* the truth, to invite others to experience it as well. But still, he does so in poetry instead of writing in prose or in philosophical writings. Poetry and metaphors are still better carriers of the mystical realms than the literal expressions of it.

Kabir is an amazing one who shines alone in many ways in the subcontinent. It's hard to do *Nirguna Bhakti* [devotion to the Divine who is *without* attributes] in poetry. It's easy to do *Saguna Bhakti* [devotion to a Divine *with* attributes], devotion to a name and form. The little Krishna, playing his flute, being naughty with the *gopis* [female friends], one can relate to in a loving way. God, coming down in flesh, like Jesus, is easy to relate to. Even in Islam, there are more *mehfil-e-naats* [gathering to recite poetry in praise of the prophet] than *mehfil-e-hamd* [gathering to recite poetry in praise of Allah]. Not that Allah is not respected or even loved, but it's so much easier to love His prophet, even though we raise our index finger and repeat many times a day that he was a person (not divine) and only a messenger. But it's much easier to love the messenger than the One who sent the message, it seems. Look at the history of hurt emotions turning into riots. They hardly ever occur when even the existence of Allah is completely denied, as in the case of the communist party and atheists, but you try to question any aspect of the messenger of the same God, and thousands come out in the streets, ready to give and take lives. To take lives of even random bystanders. That is the power of love, positive or negative, as it pours out towards the one in flesh. In Hinduism, that's *Saguna* Bhakti, which is very common. But *Nirguna* is beyond the concept of Allah even. Allah does not have a form but has detailed descriptions of his attributes. He gets angry, He loves, He creates, He listens, He guards, He punishes. *Nirguna* means not having form but also not having any attributes. So how do you show love for someone who not only does not have a body but does not even have any attributes? Shankara was the brilliant young philosopher, the greatest perhaps of Vedanta, where again God is seen as *Nirguna*. But, with all his brilliance, neither he nor Vedanta really gained popular appeal in India. But for Kabir to do loving poetry for a *Nirguna* god and then in a way that gained the kind of popularity it did with the masses, that struck a chord with the man in the street, is unparalleled.

If only the subcontinent had had a few more Kabirs. I feel like that with Bulleh Shah also, another iconoclast of formal religiosity. Or maybe we need to do what Sehdev seems to have done. To channel them within ourselves and speak from that place, on the issues that face us today. Is there not a little Bulleh Shah within us all? A little Kabir within?

But, dear Dr. Sohail, you closed with a slightly naughty request for me to talk of the spirituality of Rajneesh, or as he is lovingly called by his devotees, Osho. Coming back from California, I was surprised at how many people were familiar with the writings of Osho in Pakistan. And lovingly so. And rightly so. I do tell people, especially those who make fun of him, as he lends himself so willingly to being made fun of, to read him first. Everyone should read at least one of his books. I know you would have. Many possibly. And he has so many books. And then there are the books that are transcriptions of hundreds of his lectures.

In his introduction, let me say that I have never met anyone who had known Rajneesh personally and had anything bad to say about him. And I have met many of them. That says a lot to me. And most of the people who spent time at his Ashram in Oregon were people of above-average intelligence and had been successful in the whole capitalist race. "Been there, done that" kind of people. I was also on the West Coast, for 7 out of my 12 years in the US. In San Francisco, where many who were interested in spirituality would gravitate to. So, from personal accounts and from his writings, it's clear that he knew what he was talking about and if he came across as a nutcase, it's because that is exactly what he wanted us to see.

Osho was an iconoclast too. He broke down all our preconceptions about formal religion and spirituality and turned it into dust. He was a practitioner of Tantra and had fine-tuned the philosophy and practices of it to a very high degree. By the way, Tantra, including its spiritual sexuality, is an indigenous ancient tradition that also has roots in the Indus valley culture, where we find horned gods, yoga and Lingam/Yoni. That actually means not just Indian heritage but present-day Pakistani heritage. It remained very common in areas that were not Brahmanized and Sanskritized by the Aryans. So, Osho basically took age-old wisdom, modernized it and created something that spoke to people who were sick and tired of traditional religions and traditional moral hypocrisy and wanted to go deeper. The problem with such traditions is that either you understand it in detail and depth or from the standpoint of the traditional perspective, of course, it seems so ridiculous and outrageous. Think of the sexual art in the temples in South India. It was pure spirituality, unless seen from the 'puritanical' eyes of a Muslim or a Brahman. How could this be so?

I know that you, Dr. Sohail, know all this, but I explain a bit for others who may be reading our exchange. The point is that some of these traditions that seem ridiculous to us, that thumb their noses at the traditional morality and religions, may have tremendous wisdom behind them and may reveal something that we may be missing in our view of spirituality.

The point of all those Rolls-Royces that he wanted to show off to the world, was that it's not about not having wealth. Not at all. It's about not being obsessed with it. Like in your story of the two monks. To be able to pick it up and then drop it and go to what lies of the other side versus never to touch it but not be able to stop thinking about it.

The same goes for his view of sexuality as well. Although, in addition, as in Tantra, the use of sexuality, of coming together of opposites within oneself and then with another person, is a very coherent, ancient, complicated tradition that I would not go into the details of here. I just invite people to check his writings once at least.

So, if President Trump refined the art of trolling in politics and media, Osho fine-tuned trolling for religions and media. Oh, no, I am opening up a Pandora's Box here, I know.

OK, so, on to the totaling of religion and of spirituality by Krishnamurti. No one, I think, has done that kind of damage to formal religions and formal spirituality in recent years the way Jiddu Krishnamurti did. Again, I always ask people to read him once. Although Krishnamurti is never an easy read. But he has a tremendous way of logically taking you along and breaking down every religious bone in your God-given body. And then he would go over your body again and break down every spiritual bone as well. He was passionately against all formal spirituality and spiritual gurus. And let me write my favorite quote of him below, the one that caused havoc in my life. More on that in a minute.

"The moment you follow someone, you cease to follow the Truth."

So, in case someone reads our exchange, let me briefly tell his amazing story that beats most Hollywood, Bollywood, movie plots. So, Krishnamurti was a teenager when, along with his younger brother, he was picked up from India and brought to Europe by members of the Theosophical Society who were following psychic and spiritual signs to identify a great spiritual leader for the world. For 20 years they prepared him to lead the new spiritual order, the Order of the Star. The Theosophists had an esoteric spiritual network, with Theosophical societies all over the world (in Pakistan also). Being the leader of the World Order meant a lot of power and properties, as the Theosophists had a powerful global presence. Finally, he was in his mid-thirties and at the gathering of the Theosophists in the Netherlands, in 1929, when it was expected that the Order would finally be launched, with him heading it, he declared that he was dissolving the Orders and leaving Theosophy behind. Not just that, he said I am not your leader, because, in the search for Truth within, there are no paths, no teachers and no organized anything, including religious and spiritual organizations. His goal was to set people free of all outer gimmicks (my word) so that they could turn inwards to their own truth. He also said that he was not going to be a guru or start a new sect either. He talked to people all his life over the next 5 or 6 decades and ended up inspiring hundreds of thousands on the "pathless land of the Truth". There are those who say that the Theosophists were right in the psychic signs they saw in the boy but did not, indeed could not, know what form the spiritual revolution would take. It annihilated them, along with all other religions and spiritual movements. The Order of the Star never came up again but the Theosophists did survive and so did organized religions. But it was one very powerful blow.

So, here I was, in 1989, after having been inspired by Rumi and Hafiz and Bulleh Shah and many other Sufis and after being 'led' to a *Khanqah* of a Persian Sufi Order in San Francisco, finally contemplating joining the Sufi Order. All the signs were right. The path was just opening up beautifully. It was the

Nimatullahi Order, headed by a Persian psychiatrist, Dr. Javad Nurbakhsh, based in London at the time.

But, part of a Sufi initiation is that you surrender yourself *completely* in the hands of the Sufi Master, who does with you as he pleases, "as if with a corpse". In the initiation rite, for which I went to London, you actually take three baths and offer him your coffin, the white cloth, a symbolic death of sorts. It's a complete surrender of the will and the intellect, which I understood the deeper meaning of and the spiritual justification for, but then... but then I had Krishnamurti's writings under my pillow every night, telling me otherwise. I went through inner hell, making that choice. I *did* go through with the initiation, and followed that path extremely intensely for some years. Interestingly, exactly three years later, when I went to London to finally break out of the Order, for reasons I told you about, Dr. Nurbakhsh said, he knew all along that I was with them for a limited time. But he also said that "you can leave the Order, but you can never leave Sufism". That's like the last twist of the knife that I often think of, with a smile. Whatever that means.

Ah, this was long. From the feat of loving the formless to flirty gurus to the most solemn, serious Jiddu Krishnamurti, the destroyer of all organized faiths.

And the end of another good day and I must bid you farewell now. A pleasure exchanging ideas and experiences with you, dear Dr. Sohail.

My best regards!

Kamran

Letter No. 23

DARK SIDE OF SPIRITUALITY AND CULTISH PERSONALITIES

October 4, 2019 at 8:27 AM

Dear Kamran,

I agree with all your impressions about Kabir Das and Krishnamurti but I beg to differ with you regarding Osho.

I do not doubt that he was very intelligent and very smart and started his spiritual journey with a non-traditional noble cause but as he became popular and powerful be became obsessed with money, power and sex and started misleading the masses. He developed a personality that I call Cultish Personality. Such people can become dangerous for communities.

I have written a short essay highlighting the psychology of Cultish Personalities that I want to share with you. You need not agree with my impressions. But I wanted to share that with our readers so that they can see that we can respectfully disagree with each other in good faith.

~*~

CULTISH PERSONALITIES

While there are many genuine political and religious leaders all over the world who serve their communities and help their people liberate themselves from oppressive conditions, there are also those who create more violence than peace, more destruction than construction and more regression in their followers than progression. Such political and religious leaders have Cultish Personalities that misguide their followers. As a student of human psychology and a humanist I feel more and more people need to recognize these leaders with Cultish Personalities so that they are not misguided, manipulated, abused and exploited by them as they represent the dark side of humanity rather than the tradition of genuine enlightenment and human liberation.

When we review the biographies of these Cultish Personalities, mostly men, we come across some of the following characteristics.

1. Charm and Charisma.

These men are quite charming and display a magnetic personality that people find very impressive and attractive. These men are quite aware of their gift and believe they are "God's gift" to humanity, especially to women.

2. Ambition.

As these men become successful and popular in social, religious and political groups, they try to gain power, some through money and others through social status, as they have autocratic rather than democratic personalities. Over time their influence increases and they become more and more powerful. People start coming to visit them from far and wide.

3. Need to Control.

As these Cultish Leaders gain power, they take control of people's lives. Rather than encouraging their disciples to discover their own truth, they impose their own values, ideologies, rituals and lifestyles on their followers. They feel proud when others are converted to their political or religious ideology.

4. Abuse of Power.

As time passes and their need to control increases, they begin to exploit their disciples. They develop a hierarchy in their organization, in which there are two classes: a privileged class and an exploited class, a rich and a poor class, an abuser and an abused class. Gradually the leader acquires more and more rights and privileges: more money, more houses, more cars, more women and more luxuries of life, while the disciples sacrifice and suffer. As time passes there is more and more distance between these Cultish Leaders and their disciples. It becomes difficult for ordinary men and women to socialize with the leader. Only the privileged ones can spend time with them as they become less and less accessible to their followers. They create an atmosphere of fear and followers are worried that if they left the cult they might be penalized and persecuted, even executed.

5. *Rationalizing their Abuse of Power.*

After gaining power, control, money and status, these Cultish Leaders rationalize their abuse of power by connecting it with religious and political traditions of the community. They say to their disciples "God told me to do so" or "I had a sacred dream". These claims cannot be tested by the disciples from any objective perspective. They promote blind faith rather than rational thinking.

Some of them start performing "miracles" to amaze and amuse their followers to consolidate their power. They claim to be able to influence the weather, promise children to infertile women or say that they can magically intervene in disasters because of their "special powers". Gradually they become miracle workers and acquire some sacred status that cannot be questioned by their followers. Although the disciples are temporarily supported and reassured, the personal, social and political problems remain, as they require realistic solutions rather than illusions and fantasy solutions. Rather than becoming inspiring role models, their goal is to convert, control and exploit.

6. Losing Control

Finally, a stage comes, after a few years or decades, when these Cultish Leaders and their organizations lose control and violence and chaos erupts, either generated within the group or by their conflict with the law and social structure of their community. Disciples start to realize that they have been part of a cult and have been misguided.

When I studied the life stories of these Cultish Leaders I found it interesting that many of them started their political or religious career in a sincere and honest way and made some valid and valuable contributions to their community but as they developed more popularity, they developed a bad conscience and power corrupted them. They started their journey to find realistic solutions to social problems but gradually became leaders of a cult.

The biggest tragedy is that there are increasing numbers of simple, innocent and gullible people, some uneducated while others highly educated, who are wasting a lot of time, money and energy in promoting the destructive political and religious ideology of such Cultish Leaders. Many of them finally realize that they have been misguided and misled but sometimes it is too late, as by that time they have reached a stage of emotional, financial and ideological bankruptcy. They feel so betrayed that it takes them a long time to heal and recover. Unfortunately, some never recover.

In the 20th century, there were a number of men in America who became famous and notorious because of their Cultish Personalities. Some, like David Koresh, attracted only a few hundred disciples, while others like Sung Myung Moon, the prophet of the "Moonies" and Ron Hubbard, the guru of the Church of Scientology, have attracted millions as their disciples. Moon is well known for conducting wedding ceremonies in which thousands of men and women get married simultaneously because it has been arranged by their prophet. Sometimes the spouses do not even speak the same language. It is because to join 'Moonies' the disciples have to surrender their will, even their choice of the life partner.

One Cultish Personality that became well known in North America was Guru Rajneesh, later known as Osho, an Indian professor of philosophy. Because of his intelligence and mesmerizing personality he attracted a large number of disciples. He started teaching meditation and free sex, and thousands of Westerners who were exploring alternating lifestyles joined his ashram. Gradually local people grew critical of his philosophy and teachings and he was forced to leave India.

Rajneesh was forced to relocate to the United States where he established his own commune. For a while, he was so successful that he had accumulated, among other trappings of wealth, a fleet of 99 Rolls Royce's. However, he got into legal difficulties and was asked to leave the country.

Unfortunately, his motherland refused to take him and for a number of years, he remained homeless before his death in 1990. Some believe he was poisoned while others believe that he died of AIDS. In the years since his death, millions of people have visited his ashram in India. Interestingly the leader of the present movement is a Canadian by the name of Swami Mike, son of a British Columbian judge. According to one report, the average revenue generated in that ashram in Poona, India, is nearly 50 million dollars a year.

When we study the biographies of these Cultish Leaders, we discover that in their life story creativity, sexuality, spirituality and criminality become intimately intertwined. Truth merges with deception and eventually, the story becomes so bizarre, so surrealistic, that it becomes extremely difficult to separate fact from fiction, myth from reality.

Peacefully yours,

Sohail

Letter No. 24

POWERS OF GURUS

October 5, 2019 at 9:09 PM

Dear Dr. Khalid,

I completely agree with you on your analysis of cultish personalities. Very well done! More on why I was trying to bring out the deeper method in the madness of Rajneesh, in a few minutes. But, first, about the power trips and craziness that invariably creep into the spiritual path as one goes down the rabbit hole.

So, one of the first things that happen on Buddhist Vipassanna path is that the dreams become very vivid and lucid. This is simply because the mind gets used to frequently stopping and observing itself. To reflect on itself. On where its attention drifts to. So, while dreaming, one soon becomes aware that one is dreaming and the quality is much clearer and focused. So, within a few days of starting my meditations, I asked my teacher to tell me about dreams. He smiled and told me that attempts to understand them are just a distraction, so I needed to keep my focus on the meditations. Many traditions discourage students from early on to pay attention to exciting and attractive little breakthroughs. And even when they start having some 'powers', more established paths discourage students from using these powers, as they are seen as distractions and dangerous.

If spirituality can open up some powers within us, the powers, of course, have the potential to corrupt the most serious of seekers. But the question remains: are there any powers to know, to see, to heal that are beyond the five senses? And if so, is there a connection between having access to these powers and spiritual practices?

I have seen enough psychic phenomena to know that the mind is capable of going beyond the five senses. In Physics, I was really interested in research at the cutting edge of Particle and Quantum Physics, where the mathematical and experimental findings start presenting an underlying reality that is not that different from what the mystics had been accessing and describing in their altered mental states and 'mystical insights'. (The book that broke new ground in that direction and pretty much launched the New Age Movement was *The Tao of Physics*). So, for my Masters, I moved from the more conventional University of Minnesota to the San Francisco Bay Area. There was a JFK University in the Bay Area that offered a Graduate program in Parapsychology. By the end of that degree, one thing seemed reasonably clear, that psychic phenomena exist, even though they cannot be explained yet by any of our current established scientific theories.

These powers that seem paranormal, as we cannot explain them yet, seem to exist in every culture and in every era and can be reproduced with statistical significance in laboratory settings. This includes precognition—knowing or feeling or even having visions or dreams of something that hasn't happened yet (not possible in Einsteinian physics, unless the barrier of the speed of light can be crossed). This includes spiritual or psychic healing, mind over body, examples of which can be found all over the world. And this includes mind over matter, being able to affect objects or happenings outside of what we can do through direct contact. A man who has visions of things to come, you bring them into the laboratory and ask them to predict which card you are going to pick next, and they usually cannot perform much. And yet, the laboratory data of large trials is statistically significant enough to show that there is something beyond random guessing. It seems to happen more spontaneously though, outside of the laboratory, when it is important or meaningful to the mind of the person.

What is also clear, however, if these powers exist, is that they are not a product of what Allah opens up for a Sufi or what

Jesus allows a monk to do, or the power that Kali bestows upon her Bhakts. The spontaneously occurring paranormal phenomena are distributed across all religions and cultures, including in the former Soviet Union, among populations that did not believe in any god or spirituality. Some mental or spiritual exercises may facilitate our accessing these powers, however.

If and when an ordinary person is able to perform any task that would be termed paranormal, people, unable to explain it otherwise, tend to put him or her on a spiritual pedestal. If a person who *wants* to be seen as having spiritual powers ends up having any psychic abilities, he often goes off on a power trip. And if there are no psychic abilities involved at all, people have a need to believe that their teacher, their guru, their prophet has amazing supernatural powers. And the guru, if he is not himself generating these myths to start with, happily eats it up.

The more power, the more potential for corruption. So, instead of *"mein marna"* or moving towards selflessness, the self-image goes sky high. And that's often the beginning of a cult and the beginning of the downward spiral of the guru.

For me, for a long time, the question remained: While we are embodied in flesh, is it even possible for us to become completely selfless, to completely transcend our ego and self and hormones? Most traditions talk of their masters and prophets having gone beyond the worldly existence. Of being pure spirits. Of being *Insan-i-Kamil* (perfected beings). In California, where we had all kinds of 'gurus', with the male ones, one of my assessment criteria was to see how they would change when a beautiful woman enters the picture. It's amazing how fast their bodies and hormones kick in, how fast they get off-centered and start acting *weird*.

I deeply believe that no matter how much work we do on ourselves, psychologically or spiritually, as long as we are in the flesh, there will always be Yin and Yang within us. There is never one without the other, lurking in the shadows, close by. It is unrealistic and even unfair to expect people to be otherwise.

It's easy to talk of silly gurus. But it is interesting that many of their followers considered them prophets. Was Ron Hubbard a prophet? It depends on who is answering. To us a person might be a smart but crooked and power-hungry leader who leads hundreds, thousands astray. To his followers he may remain a prophet. For all those who committed suicide for him, of course, Jim Jones was a prophet, the greatest of all the prophets.

I was once conducting a psychological training in Lima for the United Nations staff in Central and South America. Two nationals of Haiti were describing how someone had died violently in their office and how staff got very scared of entering the office until someone was called in to cleanse the energy in the office. A third staff member, an International, working in the same office, explained how people are not very educated there and still believe in evil spirits and bad energies. And everyone laughed. I looked at the two Haitian staff members and they were smiling but were clearly embarrassed. I got so angry. I listed to the majority there, mostly Christians, the things that the Judeo-Christian and Islamic faiths hold to be true. From angels fluttering around to floating heavens to how the world and the first man were created. Talk of the death of science, logic and reasoning. It's all a matter of perspective.

Some of my most fascinating experiences while traveling, Dr. Sohail, were in North Korea. I was able to travel outside the capital, where hardly any outsiders are allowed to go. It's amazing that if everyone around us, since birth, tells us that our leader showed the whole world the ultimate truth and the right way to run a society, that becomes a reality and we would not dream of questioning the authenticity of the Great Leader.

I am oversimplifying of course. Not all spiritual groups and leaders start to lose control once they have power. Which is why it becomes an identifying characteristic, as you indicated in your letter. But then there are some leaders who know how to consolidate their power and even use violence to make sure it would spread and not be challenged. If it is to survive, some may even say, though it's hard to imagine, that anyone who questions or challenges them should just be... killed even.

So, whether Jim Jones was a prophet or not, depends on who is answering the question. Something scary about it, no?

Now, coming back to Rajneesh, I also think that towards the end he got carried away and also lost control of what his inner group was doing in Rajneeshpuram, in Oregon. He is a hard one to defend by any standards, but I still want to acknowledge the fact that with him, the relationship to money, power and sexuality was not a later underhanded development but very much a part of the upfront, coherent philosophy, very well-grounded in the age-old spiritual tradition of Tantra.

What you would find interesting, Dr. Sohail, is that when I would talk about him with my friends who had spent time with him in Oregon, I would always be challenging, though gently and respectfully, his ways and methods. When I was writing the introductory piece on him in the last letter, I was smiling to myself. They would have been pleasantly surprised.

But I have done that all my life. When talking to my American friends, I would bring out the hidden sides of Pakistan and challenge their assumptions. When talking to my friends in Pakistan, I would want them to reflect on why the Newsweek cover would show Pakistan as the most dangerous country in the world. The little that I have seen of you, I find you doing that all over the place. And I value that very much. To invite people to expand their perspective. To look at things in a different light. To know that there is always more to reality than what we are able to see and comprehend. To find, what lies hidden. To ask, what are we missing? If we see it as Yin, where lies the Yang in it? And if we see it as all pure and

Yang, where hides the Yin within it, that we need to open our eyes to, that we need to be wary of?

This broadening, and even more importantly this *shifting* of perspectives, I feel is essential to a deeper understanding of the conflicts and to the possibility of resolving these conflicts. Stepping into someone else's shoes and even before that to be able to step out of one's own shoes casually is so very hard for some nations.

So, here I was in one of the bigger cities of Pakistan, with a relatively well-educated group of people trying to do diversity training. I wanted to explore conflicting perspectives, priorities and values in different groups of people. To open up that exploration, I chose the conflict and the resulting violence around the Danish Cartoons. I asked the group to take some time to help me understand what was the value system and perspective of the people in Denmark who were supporting the publishing of the cartoons. I got nothing. I told them "you do not need to agree with them, but just to be clear on what is the value system that you are opposed to". Nothing! I pointed their attention to the increasing number of countries in Europe where people were actively supporting the magazine and even reprinting the cartoons in support of... what set of values? I insisted, "So many of them cannot all be malicious or just stupid or crazy or idiots". Out of fear or discomfort or inability, none of them were able to verbalize the other perspective.

This is dangerous. I suspect that in the decades to come, we will see more and more of these issues in the world. The conflicts are a given and not necessarily unhealthy. It's the inability to respect, or at least understand, the perspective of the other, that is alarming. The inability to be in a place from where to begin to begin to explore mutually respectful resolutions of the conflicts is scary.

I would love to hear more from you on what all you find critical to what we are up against as the world comes closer and closer together and as we have the opportunity and the necessity to interface with people with very different values, priorities and beliefs.

Again, I remain extremely grateful for the time that you are offering to continue with this conversation. Your sharing of your ideas and wisdom helps me get clarity on issues and your questions and invitations help me go deeper within my own self and my own understanding. I remain indebted to you for this exploration.

My best regards!

Kamran

Letter No. 25

PSYCHOLOGY OF SPIRITUAL ENCOUNTERS:
Psychotic Encounters

October 6, 2019 at 8:17 AM

Dear Kamran,

In my creative life I have gone through different stages. I get preoccupied with a question and then I do my research and my own reflection on my personal encounters and professional experiences and then write a chapter. A few years ago I got worried with people who say, "God talked to me". I wondered how we would know whether they are schizophrenics or mystics. How do we know whether to kiss their hands or admit them to a mental hospital? There is a psychiatric joke.

What do you call it when someone says "I talk to God"? The answer is "prayer".

And what do you call it when someone says "God talks to me"? The answer is "schizophrenia".

I wish life was as simple as this joke.

The topic is important so I have to say a lot. I will articulate my ideas in four letters. So, please do not respond until you read all four of them. Thanks!

~*~

INTRODUCTION

There was a time when spiritual encounters were only found in religious books studied by theologians and followers of different religious and spiritual traditions. But in the last century a number of psychiatrists, neurologists and psychologists have been studying spiritual encounters from a secular, humanistic and scientific point of view. Being a student of human psychology and a practicing psychiatrist I have a keen interest in those experiences and their understanding so that we can help our patients to the best of our ability and also solve the mystery of spiritual encounters.

When I review the stories of all those men and women who had spiritual encounters and claimed to be communicating with God I can easily classify them in the following groups:

PSYCHOTIC ENCOUNTERS

MYSTIC ENCOUNTERS

EPILEPTIC ENCOUNTERS

PEAK EXPERIENCES

PSYCHOTIC ENCOUNTERS

Over the decades while working as a psychiatrist in different mental hospitals in Canada I met a number of Christian men and women who experienced religious delusions and spiritual hallucinations. Some men stated "I am Jesus Christ" and some women told me "I am Virgin Mary". During their interviews, they confessed they heard God's voice telling them to do certain things in their life. Many of them followed those commands as they considered them holy. In Pakistan, I met a Muslim patient who told me "I am hearing God's voice telling me that I am Abraham and I have to sacrifice my son Ismail". To look after his son we had to ask his family members to protect the son until his father recovered. Such men and women suffered from serious mental illness. Alongside having religious delusions and hallucinations they also had thought disorder and inappropriate behavior. Many of them also suffered from paranoia and were afraid that their relatives, friends or the police were going to harm them. Some of them were even willing to be admitted to the psychiatric hospital to feel safe.

Psychiatrists believe that religious hallucinations, spiritual delusions and paranoia are part of many mental illnesses, especially schizophrenia and bipolar disorder, also known as manic depressive illness. These conditions affect nearly 1% of the general population. The rates can be higher if there is a family history of mental illnesses as they run in the families. Such illnesses are caused by biochemical changes in the brain. When the metabolism of dopamine, nor-adrenaline, 5 hydroxy-tryptamine and serotonin is disturbed in the brain it gives rise to psychotic encounters and gradual deterioration of the personality. In many cases when mental illness is diagnosed and treated early, with medications, education and psychotherapy, patients recover and lead a successful life but in some cases, the suffering is so intense, prolonged and unbearable that patients commit suicide.

One such patient was Paul that I looked after in a psychiatric hospital. He suffered from paranoid schizophrenia. He used to be preoccupied with religious and spiritual matters and as his condition deteriorated his life started to disintegrate. He, like many others who suffer from emotional problems and mental illness, had poor self-esteem. He believed he was ugly and nobody liked him. He thought he was "cursed". By the time he came to receive treatment his condition had deteriorated to such an extent that he did not respond to medications, psychotherapy, even hospitalization. One day he showed me one of his poems, which read:

Here at home

Come inside, my name is hell

Let me give you pain and agony, so you won't feel well

Over in the distance across the flames of darkness, you can hear a bell

I welcome you into my fear, I see you like it, I can tell

Two Candles of Peace

Up from God in heaven above, I was defeated and fell

Down to the stinking creation God made

I sit down here on earth a demon of hade

I hate man's soul and make him to fade

Into the night the dark gloom and shade

Death destruction is my name

And confusion and death on earth, all of it will I claim

The war pains grace in man's head...take a look around and know my name

The name of Satan is of hell, fury, furnace reign

God is but a dove, yet I am the dragon and crush his weak wing

All over each I claim suffering and life, love of greed I sing

I love the danger of battle, the screams of man in my ear I love to hear it ring

Against all spikes and stakes...God's people will I crush and fling

Come into me Satan and darken my soul

Down here in my hell inside my home

This young schizophrenic was so tormented by his psychotic encounters and religious experiences that a few months after writing this poem he committed suicide. {Ref 1}

Peacefully yours,

Sohail

P.S.: A list of all the references in these four letters is given at the end of Letter No. 28.

Two Candles of Peace

Letter No. 26

PSYCHOLOGY OF SPIRITUAL ENCOUNTERS:
Mystic Encounters

October 6, 2019 at 9:28 AM

Dear Kamran,

In this, the second letter I will focus on the Mystic Encounters.

In the last few decades I have also read stories of many Saints, Sadhus and Sants who shared their spiritual encounters in their biographies. They believe such encounters helped them develop a mystic personality and acquire spiritual enlightenment.

Maitreya, a 20th-century mystic, who claimed to be the re-birth of Buddha, in his book of revelations, *The Gospel of Peace,* writes, "The birth of every scripture seems to be tied with, and is a product of, the spiritual re-birthing of the individual, of experiencing the state which is known by a variety of names, as I said in the beginning: the Nirvanic state, enlightenment, satori, self-realization, *un-ul-haq,* illumination, re-birth, realizing the supra-mental or cosmic consciousness" {Ref 2} He shares one of his spiritual encounters in these words;

"Then about two months later, around 4.00 in the early hours of the morning I was awakened by the same divine presence, and a voice spoke to me, 'take thy pen and write. "I" shall speak to you the last book The Gospel of Peace. Start with the beginning. There was no beginning. "I" never created anything. There was no moment of birth, nor shall be one of death, of the universe. Do not be confused and write "I" never created anything outside and apart from MYSELF..." {Ref 2}

Maitreya was also known as Dr. Honda who was a well-respected professor of sociology in Toronto and served his community till his death in 1990. He led a very productive life and had many students and disciples who admired his personality and philosophy.

Dr. Honda belonged to the spiritual tradition of *hama oast*, the belief that *all that exists is God*. That tradition is different than the *hama az oast* tradition of Jews, Muslims and Christians who believe that all that exists is created by a Higher Power, a Creator, a God. There are many Saints, Sufis and Kabbalists from Christian, Muslim and Jewish traditions who, after having their spiritual encounters, dedicated their lives to serve the poor and the needy of their communities.

Many followers of spiritual traditions, whether Muslim, Christian, Jewish or Hindu, not only acquire spiritual enlightenment themselves like the Buddha, but also like to inspire others. One such 20th-century mystic was Krishnamurti who was admired by Easterners as well as Westerners. Krishnamurti was chosen by Ms. Besant of the Theosophical Society of India, who believed he had spiritual potential. He was brought to England for his spiritual grooming.

In 1922, Krishnamurti was first invited to Sydney, Australia for a Theosophical convention, where he met his old teacher Leadbeater, and later on, flew to Ojai, California, which was the beginning of a new chapter of his life. After meditating regularly, his mystical experiences became the beginning of his spiritual enlightenment. Some experiences were very painful, traumatic and bizarre. Most people around Krishnamurti were unable to fully understand those experiences but were very supportive of his mysterious mystical journey. They believed that he was experiencing the awakening of his spiritual self, generally known in the spiritual world as *kundalini* in which the person experiences a transformation of consciousness not accessible to ordinary people. One such experience Krishnamurti described to Mrs. Besant in a letter;

"The climax was reached on the 19th. I could not think, nor was I able to do anything, and I was forced by friends here to retire to

bed. Then I became almost unconscious, though I was well aware of what was happening around me. I came to myself at about noon each day. On that first day, while I was in that state and more conscious of the things around me, I had the first most extraordinary experience. There was a man mending the road; that man was myself, the pickaxe he held was myself; the very stone which he was breaking was a part of me; the tender blade of grass was my very being and the tree beside the man was myself. I almost could feel and think like the road-mender, and I could feel the wind passing through the tree and the little ant on the grass I could feel. The birds, the dust and the very noise were a part of me. Just then there was a car passing by at some distance; I was the driver, the engine and the tires; as the car went further away from me, I was going away from myself. I was in everything; or rather everything was in me, inanimate and animate, the mountain, the worm and all breathing things. All-day long I remained in this happy condition...I have seen the glorious and healing Light...I am God-intoxicated." {Ref 3}

For the next few months, Krishnamurti continued to have these mystical experiences and spiritual encounters. During a number of those episodes he became semi-conscious and his brother and friends had to look after him so that he did not hurt himself. Many times he would fall to the floor in a trance and experience seizure-like states. Gradually Krishnamurti became aware of his role in life. In February 1927, he wrote to Leadbeater,

"I know my destiny and my work. I know with certainty that I am blending into the consciousness of the one Teacher and that he will completely fill me."

In 1929 he said, *"The vision is total. To me that is liberation"*

After that liberation he resigned from the Theosophical Society and started his solitary journey as a mystic. He stated his philosophy in these words,

"I maintain that Truth is a pathless land, and you cannot approach it by any path whatsoever, by any religion, by any sect... Truth being limitless, unconditioned, and unapproachable by any path

whatsoever, cannot be organized; nor should any organization be
formed to lead or to coerce people along any particular path." {Ref 3}

After resigning from the Theosophical Society, for the next half-century, Krishnamurti traveled around the world giving lectures, meeting people from all walks of life and sharing his knowledge, experience and wisdom. He inspired thousands of people to rise above religious institutions and follow the wisdom of their own hearts. People who consulted him were not only lay people but also three generations of prime ministers of India: Jawarlal Nehru, his daughter Indira Gandhi and her son Rajev Gandhi. People who admired his knowledge and wisdom included the Dalai Lama, George Bernard Shaw, Aldous Huxley, Henry Miller, R D Laing, Joseph Campbell and many more. He was one of the most respected mystics of the 20th century.

Peacefully yours,

Sohail

Letter No. 27

PSYCHOLOGY OF SPIRITUAL ENCOUNTERS:
From Psychotic and Mystic to Epileptic

October 6, 2019 at 9:37 PM

Dear Kamran,

In this, the third letter, I will compare psychotic and mystic encounters and focus on Epileptic encounters.

COMPARING PSYCHOTIC AND MYSTIC ENCOUNTERS

When I studied the secular and scientific literature I realized that Western psychiatrists believe that psychotic and mystic encounters belong to two different categories. Psychotic experiences cause regression while the mystic encounters lead to the progression of the personality. Psychotic experiences cause emotional pain and suffering while mystic experiences lead to tranquility and peace of mind. A famous American psychiatrist Silvano Arieti compares mystics and psychotics and highlights their similarities in these words,

"Mystic experiences seem to correspond to what are called hallucinations and delusions in psychiatric terms...it is easy to confuse religious mystics with psychotic patients especially those psychotics who have hallucinations and delusions with a religious content." (Ref 4)

Alongside similarities there are also significant differences. Arieti states,

"The individual who experiences the mystical encounters has a marked rise in self-esteem and a sense of his being or becoming a worthwhile and very active person. He has been given a mission, a special insight, and from now on he must be on the move doing something important...more important than his life."

"In mystical experiences we have a tradition of auto-hypnosis. A subject puts himself into a state of a trance and projects power to the divine…The hypnosis is time-limited and totally reversible.

"The hallucinatory and delusional experiences of the schizophrenic are generally accompanied by a more or less apparent disintegration of the whole person. Religious and mystical experiences seem to result in a strengthening and enriching of the personality". {Ref 4}

While Western psychiatrists belonging to the secular tradition see psychotic and mystic encounters as distinct entities, the followers of Eastern mystic tradition believe that if psychotic experiences are supported, guided and helped they can lead to spiritual enlightenment. John White in his book *"What is Enlightenment?"* highlights different stages of spiritual enlightenment. He states that ordinary people with normal level of consciousness that he calls arthonoia, have to pass through paranoia before they reach metanoia, a stage of enlightenment. White believes that paranoia, a breakdown, can be the first step towards a breakthrough. He wrote, *"Conventional western psychologists regard paranoia as a pathological breakdown. It often is, of course, but seen from this [spiritual] perspective it is not necessarily so. Rather it can be a breakthrough…"*

Paranoia is a condition well understood by mystical and sacred traditions. The spiritual disciplines, where people practice under the guidance of guru or master, are designed to ease and quicken the passage through paranoia so that the practitioner doesn't get lost in the labyrinth of inner space and become a casualty.

Because metanoia has by large not been experienced by the founders of western psychology and psychotherapy, paranoia has not been fully understood in our culture. It is seen as an aberrant dead end rather than a necessary precondition to higher consciousness. It is not understood that the confusion, discomfort, and suffering experienced in paranoia are due entirely to the destruction of an illusion, ego. The less we cling to that illusion, the less we suffer." {Ref 5}

As practicing psychiatrists and clinicians it is important to separate psychotics from mystics as one group suffers from mental illness that might need hospitalization and treatment while the other group belongs to creative personalities that might create wisdom literature in the form of poems and plays.

It is unfortunate that many Western psychiatrists, psychologists and psychotherapists have not studied Eastern mystic literature and many Eastern mystic teachers are not well versed with Western practices of psychiatry, neurology and psychotherapy. Those who study the literature of both traditions realize that these two different disciplines sometimes use the same words and terms but mean different things reflecting different cultural traditions. Such use of words and terms can lead to major problems in communication. I will share a couple of examples to highlight this dilemma.

One of the major problems of communication between Western psychotherapists and Eastern mystic teachers is the use of the term EGO. In Western psychotherapy and psychoanalysis, Ego is the healthy part of the Self, which needs to be strengthened and developed. It reflects a mature part of the personality that can deal effectively with the instinctual pressures of the Id and the social conditioning of the Super-ego. On the other hand, Ego for Eastern mystics is the unhealthy, selfish, self-centered and arrogant part that needs to be kept under control. When we compare those two models of two traditions we see that what mystics call Ego is closer to the Id of the psychologists. James Fadiman and Robert Frager define such Ego of the mystic tradition in these words,

"The lowest level of the self, the ego, or lower personality, is made up of impulses, or drives, to satisfy desires. These drives dominate reason or judgment and are defined as the forces in one's nature that must be brought under control. The self is a product of the self-centered consciousness...the ego, the "I". The self must be transformed...that is the ideal. The self is like a wild horse; it is powerful and virtually uncontrollable. As the self becomes trained, or transformed, it becomes capable of serving the

individual...Descriptions of this level of self are similar to descriptions of the id in the psychoanalytical theory, it is closely linked to lust and aggression." {Ref 6, p 20}

Another difference between the two traditions is the concept of ego-boundaries. Psychotherapists would like those ego-boundaries of their patients to be strong to be able to deal with emotional and social crises but the mystics encourage their disciples to lose those boundaries to have spiritual encounters for their enlightenment. By dissolving ego they can get in touch with nature and feel oneness with the world in the form of self-transcendence. It seems as if in the psychotherapy tradition people are encouraged to have strong ego-boundaries for their emotional growth while in mystic tradition people are encouraged to dissolve those boundaries for their spiritual growth. It seems that both traditions have a common goal of personal growth and search of personal truth but they use different vocabularies and practices reflecting their respective traditions. James Gordon highlights the differences between Western and Eastern concepts, Freudian psychoanalysis and mysticism, in these words,

"Freud had postulated a tripartite division of mental functioning. In the centre was the ego, mediating between the instinctual demands of the id and the harsh familial and cultural imperatives and prohibitions that were internalized in the super-ego. One of the goals of psychoanalysis was the reclamation for the ego of the territory previously governed by the id and the super-ego. For psychoanalysis, the ego represented the highest aspect of development... the ego was the realm of sanity... and the confusion of the inner and the outer world was the hallmark of psychosis... Freud noted that this inclination to abolish the boundaries of the ego and merge with what was outside was connected with religious experience. He said he could understand the appeal of the 'oceanic feeling' the unbroken connectedness to the world. But he felt obliged to remind readers that it was regressive. The vestige of a lesser rather than a more highly developed consciousness...

For the mystics the formation of ego was a necessary stage rather than a goal, as much as a barrier as an achievement... There are some persons who embark on and complete the voyage of ego dissolution and transformation on their own. Most often, a guide seems to be necessary. The guide has experienced the process and is now prepared to aid others in undergoing it. In the East, he is called a Master. The relationship between him and his disciples provides the motive for transformation, and reassurance and protection during the process." {Ref 7}

EPILEPTIC ENCOUNTERS

While working in emergency units of different hospitals I also came across a number of patients who had very unusual symptoms of depersonalization, de-realization and *deja vu*. Some of them also developed religious preoccupation and even had conversion reactions. Some of them even had religious delusions and spiritual hallucinations and were diagnosed as schizophrenics. They were treated with anti-psychotic medications by their doctors but the condition did not improve. When we did EEG, we discovered that they suffered from Temporal Lobe Epilepsy and when treated with anti-epileptic medications their condition improved.

I will talk more on the Epileptic encounters and Temporal Lobes in the next letter.

Peacefully yours,

Sohail

Letter No. 28

PSYCHOLOGY OF SPIRITUAL ENCOUNTERS:

Of Temporal Lobe and Peak Experiences

October 7, 2019 at 6:54 PM

Dear Kamran,

In this, fourth letter, I will focus on the role of the Temporal Lobes in spiritual experiences and creative encounters.

THE ROLE OF THE TEMPORAL LOBES IN SPIRITUAL AND CREATIVE ENCOUNTERS

While studying different forms of epilepsy a number of neurologists have discovered that temporal lobes are related to spiritual encounters and creative experiences. Human beings have a wide range of mystical and creative experiences depending upon the sensitivity of their temporal lobes.

Dr. Robert Buckman, in his book *"Can We Be Good Without God?"* {Ref 8} presents an enlightening review of the literature and research done by a number of neurologists. He brings to our attention that the temporal lobes play a significant role in the perceptions and experiences that we associate with creative and mystic encounters. He describes that the left lobe deals with "language and motor skills" while the right lobe deals with 'the person's perception of reality and of himself and herself ...' {Ref 7, p. 115}. Many of these changes have been proven by the EEG [electroencephalograph] invented in the 1940s and since then used in studying epileptic patients and sleep problems in normal people.

Based on EEG studies, Buckman highlights that human beings can be divided into three groups depending upon the sensitivity of the temporal lobes.

1. People who have highly sensitive temporal lobes suffer from temporal lobe epilepsy as they have spontaneous firing of the neurons of the temporal lobe. Dr. Hughlings Jackson studied those epileptics and discovered that their auras, hallucinations and out of body experiences were not much different than what was reported by Saints in their mystic encounters. Prior to epileptic seizures the auras... "include some very particular sensations and experiences. These may include any (or several) of the following: auditory hallucinations {hearing voices}, *deja vu* [the feeling of having seen something before], visual hallucinations, experiencing funny smells, a feeling of particular peace, a sensation of deep understanding or of profound and significant knowledge and a feeling of being outside one's body" {*Ref 7, p. 119*}. One such example was the famous Russian writer, Fyodor Dostoevsky, who suffered from temporal lobe epilepsy and shared his experiences in his writings, stating "...all of the forces of life gathered convulsively all at once to the highest attainable consciousness...and then a scene suddenly as if something were opening up in the soul: an indescribable, an unknown light radiated, by which the ultimate essence of things was made visible and recognizable. {*Ref 8, p. 120*}. Based on the experiences of temporal lobe epileptics some neurologists wonder if we had had EEG we might have discovered that some mystics in history, like Joan of Arc, might have suffered from temporal lobe epilepsy.

Dr. Wilder Penfield did extensive studies of the brain. When he stimulated the left side of the brain he saw involuntary movements of different parts of the body. "But when he stimulated the temporal lobe on the right side, there was no movement of any part of the body. Instead the patients reported a wide variety of significant experiences, perceptions and/or feelings. The phenomena reported were basically the same as the auras accompanying temporal lobe seizures... feelings of great peace, of deep understanding, of consciousness of another being..." {Ref 8, p. 122}

2. People who have temporal lobes more sensitive than average but less sensitive than those of epileptics have creative encounters and become poets and artists and actors as it is easy for them to enter imaginary worlds and create characters or play roles of other people by getting involved in "...drama, poetry and other creative acts: activities that require the person to 'go into' another world or another mode are associated with high temporal lobe scores." {Ref 8, p. 133}

3. In people who have average temporal lobes and do not suffer from temporal lobe epilepsy and are not poets or actors, stimulation of their temporal lobes by electrodes in the laboratory, produces similar experiences. Rather than having epileptic seizures, they have perceptual and sensory experiences similar to the ones shared by mystics. When M. A. Persinger did experiments on volunteers by stimulating their temporal lobes he noticed they experienced "...a feeling of peace, of serenity, of being one with nature and often of being in the presence of another consciousness (another being). Some people felt that they were near the presence of aliens. Others experienced deeply spiritual or religious feelings. Some reported that they were in the presence of god, and some heard his voice." {Ref 8, p. 125}

One of the well-respected neurologists of our time V. S. Ramachandran developed some insights in the relationship of temporal lobes and religious and spiritual encounters.

V. S. Ramachandran explored the neural basis of hyper-religiosity seen in TLE [Temporal Lobe Epilepsy] using galvanic skin response, which correlates with emotional arousal, to determine whether the hyper-religiosity seen in TLE was due to an overall enhanced emotional response, or if the enhancement was specific to religious stimuli {Ref 9}. By presenting subjects with neutral, sexually arousing and religious words while measuring GSR, Ramachandran was able to show that patients with TLE showed enhanced emotional responses to the religious words, diminished responses to the sexually charged words and normal responses to the neutral words. These results suggest that the medial temporal lobe is specifically involved in generating some of the emotional reactions associated with religious words, images and symbols. {Ref 10}

How do we understand these spiritual and creative encounters from a scientific and neurological point of view? Julian Jaynes tried to explain those encounters based on his theory of Right/Left Brain functioning. He believes that the temporal lobe of the Left Brain deals with language while the temporal lobe of the Right Brain deals with sensory, perceptual and aesthetic experiences. He explains that creative and mystic experiences originate in the Right Brain and when those messages are sent to the left Brain, the Left Brain does not own them and feels as if those messages came from the outside and, depending upon the personality and culture, are interpreted as coming from angels, spirits or God rather than their unconscious mind. (Ref 11)

Dr. Robert Buckman concludes his discussion by stating his opinion that "If the limbic system is activated by means of the temporal lobe, a person will have an experience of the spiritual or divine type. God is... literally... a state of mind." {Ref 8, p. 144}

After reviewing the literature it seems to me that although creative and mystic encounters are universal and men and women from all traditions experience them but the interpretation of those experiences depends upon the beliefs of those who experience them. The more the secular traditions become established, the more we are able to see spirituality as part of humanity.

BARRIERS OF LANGUAGE AND CULTURE

The more we study psychotic, spiritual and creative encounters, the more we realize that spiritual human experiences are mystified because we still do not have proper words and terms to describe them. Because of different cultural traditions, different communities give them different meanings. People following a religious and spiritual tradition connect such experiences with the concepts of God and angels while followers of a secular tradition relate such experiences to our unconscious minds.

I am of the opinion that it is important for us to separate the experiences from their interpretations. As we evolve as human beings and disciplines of science, psychology, neurology and philosophy grow, we would have a better understanding of such extra-ordinary experiences and we would be able to decrease human suffering and increase the quality of our lives so that we can grow and evolve to the next stage of human evolution.

CREATIVE AND PSYCHOTIC ENCOUNTERS

When I studied the biographies of creative personalities whether poets or painters, novelists or philosophers, I discovered that some of them suffered from temporal lobe epilepsy while others had psychotic encounters. Edgar Allan Poe and Fyodor Dostoevsky had temporal lobe epilepsy while Virginia Woolf, Sylvia Plath, Vincent Van Gogh and Ernest Hemingway felt so distressed and depressed because of their psychotic experiences that they committed suicide. There are a number of neurologists and geneticists who are testing their hypothesis that the gene of insanity and creativity is the same and depending upon the support or criticism they receive from their families and communities, people either have nervous breakdowns or creative breakthroughs or both.

PEAK EXPERIENCES

In the twentieth century as the frontiers of science and human psychology expand, many scientists and psychologists are bringing to our awareness that spirituality does not belong only in churches, mosques and monasteries; it can be part of our day to day life. They highlight that spiritual experiences are not restricted only to mystics; rather, they can be experienced by anyone in special circumstances. Psychologists like Abraham Maslow have been collecting observations, findings and conclusions that "can be accepted as real by clergymen and atheists alike" {Ref 12, p. 54}. Maslow was of the opinion that the segregation of sacred and profane, saint and sinner, mystic and pragmatist, is artificial and unnatural. In trying to reclaim spirituality as part of humanity, he wrote, "I want to demonstrate that spiritual values have naturistic meaning, that they are not the exclusive possession of organized churches, that they do not need supernatural concepts to validate them, that they are within the jurisdiction of a suitably enlarged science, and that, therefore, they are the general responsibility of all mankind." {Ref 12, p. 4}

Maslow believed that ordinary men and women can have extraordinary experiences, and unusual things can happen in usual circumstances. He named those special experiences *"peak experiences"* and described a number of characteristics of these experiences that can occur spontaneously in the life of any layperson, poet, intellectual, scientist, artist or religious person. Peak experience, Maslow believed, can occur while watching a sunset, playing with one's grandchild, making love, composing a poem or contemplating the mysteries of the universe, although certain types of practices and disciplines, like meditation, might make the likelihood of those experiences more probable and more frequent. He explained that those human experiences are labeled as spiritual/religious/mystic because of the belief system of that individual, community and culture. By calling them *peak experiences* and highlighting that a religious belief was not a prerequisite to having them, Maslow tried to secularize the spiritual and religious world. He shared one of the features of *peak experiences* in these words, "...in a peak experience such emotions as wonder, awe, reverence, humility, surrender and even worship before the greatness of the experience are often reported." {*Ref 12*}

Maslow also studied the changes in people's personalities after they had those special *peak experiences.* He observed that in some people those experiences had a profound impact on people's lifestyles. He wrote, "...the peak experiencer becomes more loving and more accepting and he becomes more spontaneous and honest and innocent." {*Ref 12, p. 76*}

It seems as if peak experiences help us become better human beings.

CONCLUDING COMMENTS

In these letters, I have tried to show that all those people who have spiritual encounters belong to four groups.

People who belong to the first group have psychotic encounters and suffer from a mental illness, experiencing religious hallucinations and spiritual delusions. They need psychiatric treatment with medications, education and psychotherapy to control their symptoms and improve their quality of life.

People who belong to the second group choose to have spiritual encounters to achieve spiritual enlightenment. They use auto-hypnosis to put themselves in a trance. Before they reach enlightenment, they go through a painful phase of emotional suffering. In some traditions a mystic teacher is recommended to help disciples and students go through that painful phase with some ease. John White highlights that some seekers of enlightenment become a casualty by having a breakdown and never reaching a breakthrough.

People belonging to the third group suffer from temporal lobe epilepsy as their temporal lobes fire spontaneously. They need to be treated by anti-epileptic medications. Studies of temporal lobes showed us that temporal lobes are not only involved in spiritual encounters but also in creative encounters of scientists, artists and mystics.

People belonging to the fourth group are ordinary people who have extra-ordinary peak experiences in their day to day lives by getting in touch with nature and creative aspects of their personality.

Recent advances in the fields of psychiatry, neurology and psychology are forcing the followers of all religious, spiritual, secular and scientific traditions to review their positions. On the one hand, on the left, more and more enlightened atheists and agnostics are realizing that spiritual encounters are genuine human experiences that can be studied by scientists and psychologists. On the other hand, on the right, more and more enlightened believers, followers of Muslim, Christian, Hindu and Jewish traditions are becoming aware that to have spiritual encounters people do not need to believe in any God or religion. These experiences are related to our temporal lobes and a reflection of the creative aspect of personality that all of us have, some more than others.

Albert Einstein believed that we need to encourage those experiences as they help us in having creative and mystical encounters commonly experienced by scientists, mystics and artists. He wrote,

"It is very difficult to elucidate this [cosmic religious] feeling to anyone who is entirely without it....The religious geniuses of all ages have been distinguished by this kind of religious feeling, which knows no dogma....In my view, it is the most important function of art and science to awaken this feeling and keep it alive in those who are receptive to it." {Ref 9}

Albert Einstein, a scientist, like J Krishnamurti, a mystic, and Abraham Maslow, the psychologist, believed that to have mystical experiences and spiritual encounters we need not believe in any religion or sect. An atheist and an agnostic can have as profound a mystical experience as a dedicated Christian, Muslim, Hindu or a Jew. Spiritual encounters are part of the creative side of our personalities. The more we become creative the more we develop higher consciousness and can appreciate fine arts. Such special consciousness is well developed in all creative people whether poets or painters, artists or philosophers, reformers or revolutionaries and because of such consciousness these creative personalities lead humanity to the next stage of human evolution. It is unfortunate and sad to see that the creative minority has to suffer and offer sacrifices for the growth and evolution of the majority. Lucky are the communities and cultures that value such a creative e minority. In the words of Arnold Toynbee, "*To give a fair chance to potential creativity is a matter of life and death for any society. This is all important because the outstanding creative ability of a fairly small percentage of the population is mankind's ultimate capital asset...*" {Ref.13}

REFERENCES

1. Sohail K. *From Islam to Secular Humanism* Abbeyfield Publishers Canada 2001

2. Maitreya *Gospel of Peace* Universal Way Publications Canada 1988

3. Jayakar Papal *Krishnamurti...A Biography* Harper and Rowe Publishers New York 1985

4. Arieti Silvano *Interpretation of Schizophrenia* Basic Books New York USA 1974

5. White John *What is Enlightenment?* Jermey Tarcher Inc Los Angeles USA 1984

6. Fadiman James and Frager Robert *Essential Sufism* Castle Books New Jersey USA 1997

7. Gordon James *The Golden Guru...The Strange Journey of Bhagwan Shree Rajneesh* Stephen Greene Books USA 1987

8. Buckman Robert *Can We Be Good Without God?* Viking Books Canada 2000

9. Ramachandran VS *Phantoms in the Brain ...Probing the mysteries of the Human Mind* Harper Collins Publishers USA 1998

10. Wikipedia: Temporal Lobe Epilepsy

11. Jaynes Julian *The Origin of Consciousness in the Breakdown of the Bicameral Mind* Mariner Books 1990

12. Maslow Abraham *Religions, Values and Peak Experiences* Penguin Books England 1970

13. Arieti Silvano *Creativity...The Magic Synthesis* Basic Books Inc. Publisher New York 1976

Dear Kamran,

I hope these four letters give you the highlights of my readings and reflections on the subject. Now I will look forward to your comments.

Peacefully yours,

Sohail

144

Letter No. 29

FROM PERSONAL GOD TO THE SACRED WONDER BEHIND ALL CREATION

October 7, 2019 at 9:37 PM

Dear Dr. Sohail,

During my academic years, from Physics to Philosophy to Parapsychology to Clinical Psychology to Spirituality, while I have come across many of these concepts, I have never seen them put together so well and presented so softly and coherently and with such a high degree of intellectual integrity. This is a great service to all who would read it. I wish one could make this a required reading for all high school students, indeed all people, especially in our part of the world. I am deeply honored that you shared it with me. Thanks!

There was a time when people would pray to and have deep spiritual connections with Greek and Norse gods. Today, Hercules, son of Zeus and Thor, son of Odin, are popular Hollywood characters, in the same category as Iron Man. So, here I was, wearing a Thor T-shirt, as I was working on some videos with a very creative young director. Looking at my T-shirt, he said, "don't you think Dr. Kamran that eventually all religions will end up like that? There were people who would live their lives swearing by the truth and reality of these gods". His question comes back to me often.

To those who believed in Thor as a god, if they were having simultaneous firings in their temporal lobes, they could easily see him appearing to them and talking to them. Or experience being Thor themselves. The same physical condition in the mind of someone in Tibet would not be experienced through an image of Thor but as the Dalai Lama or the Buddha. And for someone entrenched in Native American mythology, it could not be the Buddha but perhaps Hiawatha or the spirit of his power animal talking to him and guiding him.

I remember my Islamiyat teacher getting upset with me when, in my youth, I asked him why the characters and stories of the Middle Eastern religions never showed up in the religions of the Indians or the Chinese or, my favorite mythology when I was young, the Native American myths. Since God was the same in the Bible and in the Quran, the same stories and characters show up to teach us particular lessons. But if God was still the same in China, why would the same stories and characters not show up to teach us the same particular lessons? And I was silly enough to actually ask my religion teacher about it. Luckily those were relatively tolerant times.

From 1989 to 1992, I did not have visions but in my dreams I used to be guided by Dr. Javad Nurbakhsh, the Sufi master of the Nimatullahi Order. And before that I had dreams of the Prophet himself as well, appearing with a tremendous feeling of grace and peace. To my Christian friends it would be dreams of the Christ, as that image would embody, would clothe best the feeling that they were experiencing.

Of the mystics, yes, Joan of Arc would see the Christ. And the tremendously intense experiences that Saint Theresa had with the Christ. And the Sufi masters with Hazrat Ali and Allah. And so on.

But get this… a few decades ago, I had an amazingly powerful dream where the one guiding me was… well it was Master Yoda! The dream had all the makings of a spiritual guiding dream except that the teacher this time was not a Sufi but, Yoda. Now the fact is that out of all the present day mythological Hollywood figures, in my mind, Yoda comes closest to a Zen Master or a spiritual guru. Later, of course, I found out how Joseph Campbell, one of the most popular Anthropologists of recent times, spent so much time at the Skywalker Ranch with George Lucas when they were creating what they described as a "mythology for the modern age", Star

Wars. They borrowed heavily from all kinds of spiritual traditions.

Talking of Campbell, I consider him to be a deeply spiritual person. Mythology was not an intellectual pursuit for him. You could see the experiential base, the excitement and the childlike twinkle in his eyes when he would compare spiritual concepts from around the world. He knew it on an experiential level. And he very clearly said that I have no need for a belief or a faith in a personal, anthropomorphic [human-like] god. He did, however, talk about the pantheistic sense of the Divine in all of creation that Einstein and Maslow talk of. In fact, in describing his spiritual experiences, he uses Maslow's term of Peak Experiences, that you describe so well in your letter.

So, yes, perhaps, now that we are not living locked up in our own separate villages and tribes, humanity slowly may switch to broader terms that do not only borrow from these or those teaching stories but are more universal. Alternatively, if we can recognize the underlying common experiences and truths and wear our stories, our characters, our religious terminology as light garbs that we cover our bodies with, that could work too. As long as we are not overly attached to the name and form.

It is odd for me to hear the Buddhists talk in increasingly religious terms in the world today. If anyone stuck to the *experience* in meditations, without being lured into giving it any meaning or form, it was the Buddha. He would not answer any metaphysical questions. Later there were all kinds of ideas, mostly Sanskrit, that got added to his mental techniques and meditations. There is a story of a Buddhist monk who after practicing *Vipassanna* for decades finally has the most glorious image of the Buddha appear before him. He was so excited that he went to his teacher and joyfully reported what had happened to him and what he had seen. The teacher waved him away, saying, "just stay with the breath and don't worry… it will go away". And I know you know of the old Zen teaching, that became the name of a popular book also, *If You Meet Buddha on the Road, Kill Him.*

Rumi wrote, (and I paraphrase...) "I met a monk walking upon my path. We do the same work, I told him. We suffer the same."

So, again, if only we would not get stuck in the language and images, in the name and form, in the *Nama-Rupa*, if we could only wear our religions lightly...

The connection of mystical experiences to psychology, you have summarized so well that I feel nothing could or indeed should be added to it.

My gratitude and best regards!

Kamran

Letter No. 30

MYTHOLOGY AND JOSEPH CAMPBELL

October 8, 2019 at 8:19 AM

Dear Kamran,

I feel honored that a scholar like you was satisfied with my humble attempt to capture the essence of spirituality in a few pages.

I am so amazed and amused that you were inspired by Joseph Campbell. There was a time I was intrigued by him. So I ordered a book not knowing that there was also a poet by the same name. So I got a book of the wrong Joseph Campbell. Then I ordered the book of the Joseph Campbell I was looking for. I wanted to read the summary of his interviews and lectures that he gave to the Public Broadcast in the USA before he died.

After reading his lectures and interviews I wrote a long essay that I want to share with you.

After reading the essay you can share your comments. In one of your letters, I would also like you to summarize your ideas that you presented in your lecture to Family of the Heart. I am sure our readers will learn a lot from your ideas and ideals.

Peacefully yours,

Sohail

JOSEPH CAMPBELL: A PHILOSOPHER OF MYTHOLOGY

Joseph Campbell was a three-dimensional intellectual. He was able to integrate his studies of human psychology, sociology, anthropology, history and mysticism into his discipline of mythology. He was like a mythological old man, sitting on the top of a mountain watching the caravans of humanity pass by. He was like an ancient story-teller who knew the folk tales of all cultures and enjoyed sharing them with the coming generations.

Joseph Campbell, alongside being an accomplished intellectual, was also a kind man. He had the mind of a philosopher and the heart of a mystic. He was a gentle, peaceful and compassionate person. He accepted rather than judged people. That is why people from all walks of life, from different religious and cultural traditions, were attracted to him. He had great insights into the human condition and also had the gift to present very complicated and sophisticated concepts in layman's language because he knew the power of myth and metaphor.

He was one of the few intellectuals of the twentieth century who built bridges between science and spirituality. He had a scientific attitude towards mysticism and a mystic attitude towards science. He tried to study human history from a mythological point of view.

Since Joseph Campbell has talked and discussed dozens of subjects in his lectures and interviews, I will just focus on a few issues that I found quite interesting and fascinating.

DOMAIN OF MYTHOLOGY

Joseph Campbell believed that mythology deals with the mysteries of human condition especially focusing on the relationship between human beings and the universe. Over the centuries human beings have been trying to explore and understand their mysterious relationship with their environments. It has not been easy for many people to comprehend mythology as it goes far beyond the realm of logic and rationality and concepts. It deals with the essence of life. Mythology deals with issues that the rational mind does not fully comprehend. It is because mythology uses the language of symbols and images and metaphors, which touches human beings at a deeper level than rational and logical thinking. Human mythology has two parts, a personal and a collective. Personal myths are experienced through visions and dreams. That is why the waking rational mind has difficulties understanding the night dreams as well as nightmares because they deal with the unconscious aspects of the personality. Sigmund Freud tried to explore those aspects of the human psyche and created his masterpiece *Interpretation of Dreams*. On the other hand, collective myths are expressed by art and literature and folklore. That is the area where Carl Jung made his significant contributions by interpreting images and stories of folklore in his book *Man and His Symbols* and introducing his concept of the collective unconscious. Joseph Campbell acknowledged the contributions of Freud and Jung but felt that as he got older he felt closer to Jung than Freud as he was fascinated by mythology and believed that "...the first function of a mythology is to awaken and maintain in the individual a sense of wonder and participation in the mystery of this finally inscrutable universe." *{Ref 2, p. 17}*

1.   BIRTH OF HUMAN BEINGS

Joseph Campbell believed that human beings, *Homo sapiens,* were born when animals reached a stage in evolution when they could walk on two feet and develop their brains. With the increase of the size of brains they could experience a transformation of consciousness. Such transformation made it possible for human beings to create mythology. It is amazing to note that such a change took place in many parts of the world at the same time. Campbell stated, "Now we come to later *Homo sapiens,* Cro-Magnon man. This order of the human species appears around 30, 000 to 40, 000 B.C. and appears not only in Europe, where he was first discovered, but also in Southeast Asia and in two or three other places, as though there was a parallel evolution taking place." {Ref 1, p. 10}

As human beings evolved they created human civilizations. The early signs of those civilizations are found by archeologists who discovered ruins of cities like Mohenjo-Daro in India and other parts of the world. Those cities were erected a few thousand years B.C. As civilizations became more sophisticated human beings created languages, arts and religions. They also became aware of cycles in nature around them and the relationship of those cycles with human life. One such example was the "recognition of the equivalence of the menstrual and the lunar cycles. This would be the first inkling we have of recognition of counterparts between the celestial and earthly rhythms of life." {Ref 1, p. 13}

With the development of a microscope and a telescope, human beings were able to make accurate observations and predictions of stars, moons and suns and developed the lunar and the solar calendars.

2. MATRIARCHAL / PATRIARCHAL MYTHOLOGIES

Joseph Campbell, in his lectures, discussed different cultures, mythologies and civilizations throughout history. He believed that there was a time when human civilizations were matriarchal. In India, archeologists have discovered an old temple nearly 4000 B.C where the courtyard was of the shape of the vagina of a cow. People of that part of the world, in those times, considered cow as the goddess and her milk as sacred milk. The cow was the symbol of mother god and her four feet the four corners of the compass. Even today we find sacred cows wandering around in the streets of India. Researchers like Marija Gimbutas [author of *Goddesses and Gods of Old Europe*] have also shown that even in Europe during 7000-3500 B.C, the matriarchal mythologies were more prevalent. The expressions like mother tongue and mother-land still remind us of those times.

Gradually the mother goddesses went in the background and male gods took over and the societies became patriarchal. This change took place after Zeus and Yahweh, the male gods, became popular. Such a change also promoted tribal thinking because Yahweh was not only considered to be a god but also the *only* god of Israel. According to that mythology, gods of other communities were considered evil and called devils. Campbell brings to our attention that "Yahwehist monotheism says, "There is no other God in the world. Those others are devils." *{Ref 1, p. 85}.* Over the centuries, followers of that tradition, whether Christians or Muslims wanted to spread the message of their God to other nations either by preaching or by declaring holy wars.

3. EASTERN AND WESTERN MYTHOLOGIES

Joseph Campbell shared that the Eastern and Western traditions are different as they are the outcome of different mythologies of the world. Eastern traditions are the products of the teachings of Buddha, Confucius and Lao-tzu, all three living nearly 500 B.C. Buddha focused on finding nirvana, one's own truth and following the 'right path'. Confucius focused on the philosophy of social responsibility and Taoism highlighted the relationship of human beings with nature. *{Ref 1, p. 122}*

In the Eastern mythology, spiritual tradition believes that the Divine exists in all of us and all human beings can have a mystical experience. Such tradition is closer to the Native American tradition. Native Americans also believe that all human beings are capable of discovering their own spirituality through dreams and visions. Native Indians believe that God is the Great Mystery of the universe.

As compared to the Eastern tradition, the Western tradition believes that God is the creator and human beings are the creation. Western mythology also believes that God is the Master and human beings are the subjects and their role is to praise and worship their Lord. Campbell believed that the king concept of God was first presented by Darius in 1000 B.C in the Near East. Darius presented God as the king of the kings and believed that human beings were the slaves. Such a concept became popular in the Middle East and was adopted by Judaism, Christianity and Islam. Campbell highlights that these religious traditions have not been respectful and accepting of religious and spiritual traditions of other cultures.

Campbell believed that people in the West have inherited two traditions, tradition of the Bible and that of Aristotle, one of the Greek philosophers. Greek Philosophers were the first ones who, in their philosophy presented Human Beings as primary and gods as secondary. Greek Philosophers not only created a rational system of thinking, which helped humanity in establishing sciences, but also developed a humanistic philosophy.

According to that philosophy, gods became the echoes of the human psyche. Humanistic philosophy believes that human beings created gods rather than gods created human beings. Such a philosophy revolutionized how human beings experienced the world around them. As the Greek philosophy developed it challenged the myths of the Western world.

4. MYTHOLOGY, RELIGION AND SCIENCE

Joseph Campbell considered religion a misinterpretation of mythology. When people cannot fully experience the spiritual dimension of life and comprehend the abstract, they rely on the concrete interpretations of symbols, images, metaphors and scriptures. Such literal interpretations lead to religious leaders and institutions that misguide people. The religious tradition judges people and declares them sinners. On the other hand, the mystic tradition accepts people and encourages them to get in touch with their deeper selves. Campbell believed that when communities lose touch with mythologies, they develop ideologies. Campbell highlighted that one of the basic differences of religion and mysticism is the concept of good and bad, right and wrong, sin and virtue. He said, "The mystical dimension is beyond good and evil. The ethical dimension is in the field of good and evil. One of the problems in our religions lies in the fact that it accents, right from the start, the good and evil problem." {Ref 1, p. 22}

Joseph Campbell did not see any conflict between science and mythology, as he stated, "I would say that there is no conflict between mysticism, the mystical dimension and its realization, and science" {Ref 1, p. 46}. He believed that the science and mythology of 2000 BC were in harmony, but the mythology of 2000 BC is in conflict with the science of 2000 AD because contemporary mythology has not kept in touch with contemporary science. "Your mythology, your imagery, has to keep up with what you know of the universe, because what it has to do is put you in accord with the universe as known, not as it was known in 2000 B.C in the Near East." {Ref 1, p. 22}. He believed that new mythology is developed when creative people come up with new symbols, images and metaphors that embrace the contemporary understanding of life.

Joseph Campbell thought that in the contemporary world there is not only conflict between science and religion but also between different religions. He stated that even followers of Jewish, Christian and Islamic traditions are not able to live peacefully with each other in the Middle East, as they are insisting on their own tradition and not respecting other traditions.

He states that in the mystic tradition of the East, people are encouraged to focus on the essence, on the experience, rather than the method. He praised Dalai Lama, who in his speech in America had encouraged his listeners to follow their own path hoping that their sincerity will eventually lead them to their spiritual truth. "Dalai Lama said, 'Keep up your practice. The results do not happen fast: there is no instant realization. And as you practice, you will become aware of a change of consciousness. Do not become attached to your method, for when your consciousness changes, you will recognize that all the methods are intending the one goal.' That is the song mythology sings." {Ref 1, p. 63}

5. EAST AND WEST LEARNING FROM EACH OTHER

Joseph Campbell felt that while Eastern people can learn from the Western tradition of science and humanism, Western people can also learn from Eastern spirituality and the disciplines of yoga and meditation. He discussed his understanding of yoga and meditation as a way to discover one's own truth. He explained that by comparing the human mind to a pond. He shared that when pebbles are thrown in the pond, the images remain shattered. But when the pond is still, the surface becomes a mirror and one can see clear reflections. He stated that yoga helps people to clear their minds from the haphazard thought patterns of the brain, reacting to outside stimuli, and develop a peaceful state, in which people can see and experience the reflections of their inner self and get in touch with their true self, their true nature and then realize that their true nature has similarities with the true nature of other humans as well as the universe. Such truth and consciousness is beyond words and forms. Joseph Campbell shared, "This consciousness that throws up forms and takes them back again, throws up forms and takes them back again. And then you can realize that you are one with the consciousness in all beings...This is the ultimate mystic experience on earth." {Ref 1, p. 27}. In this way the individuality of human beings gets in touch with the universality of humanity and universe as "the function of yoga is to release us from the time-space commitment, introduce us to the transcendent" {Ref 1, p.134}. But such experiences are mystical and are beyond words and languages and rational workings of the mind. So they can be *experienced* but are very difficult to explain or describe to others. One of the ways mystics share those experiences with others is through symbols and metaphors that give rise to folklore and wisdom literature.

6. LIFESTYLE

Alongside being impressed by Joseph Campbell's philosophy I am also impressed by his lifestyle. He was one of those creative people who could rise above the temptations of the materialistic world and focus on his own passions and dreams. He was quite dedicated to his creative work. His commitment to his teaching and learning helped him deal with issues that others find stressful. In that way, he seemed to have a spiritual and mystical approach to life. Michael Toms wrote, "Joseph took pride in the fact that he never did anything primarily for money. This was because he derived so much fulfillment from doing just what was important to him, what was meaningful...Once, when I was speaking with him about his capacity to forgo the usual trappings of the materialistic mainstream, he replied by saying that he had luck. I thereby asked, " isn't there a myth that says you create your own luck?" laughing loudly, he retorted, "That is not only a myth."

7. INTIMATE RELATIONSHIPS

Alongside his personal life, I was also impressed by his attitude towards intimate relationships in general and his marriage in particular. He was one of those few creative people who had discovered a balance between his creative and family lives. He was married to his wife for almost half a century. He believed that marriage goes through two stages. The first stage is romantic and lustful but in the later years it develops a spiritual dimension and those people who cannot develop this spiritual dimension in their long term intimate relationships, the relationships usually fall apart. He stated, "Then there comes a time when those vital energies aren't there, but at the same time, there is an awakening of a spiritual relationship. When that does not happen, you see people getting divorced." {Ref 2, p. 128}. He believed that the secret of a lasting loving relationship is the attitude where both parties feel that they are giving to the relationship and building it together rather than giving to the other partner resentfully. He said, "And when you are giving, you are not giving to the other person; you are giving to the relationship" {Ref 2, p. 127}. When people happily contribute to the relationship then they grow together.

8. MEANING IN LIFE

Joseph Campbell had an existentialist approach towards life. He believed that life did not have any intrinsic meaning, but it had many meanings depending upon what meaning we create for our lives. He believed that we were all free as human beings to choose our lifestyle and follow our own bliss. And following one's own bliss is a mixed blessing. It is like walking on a razor's edge because, on one hand, nobody has done it before, but it is also the secret of leading a creative and successful life. Obviously he had found his own bliss as he followed the suggestion of William Blake, "Arise and drink your bliss! For everything that lives is holy". {Ref 2, p. 17}

9. APPRECIATING METAPHORS

The most important thing I learnt from Joseph Campbell was to appreciate metaphors, as they not only help us understand our dreams but also learn from folklore and scriptures as they all use the language of symbols and metaphors. He believed that the stories of the Garden of Eden and the Flood of religious scriptures need not be perceived as concrete realities, as they were mythological metaphors. He explained many religious symbols in lay man's language. For example, Joseph Campbell explained that the symbol of cross consists of four corners and one center. The four corners represent two sets of opposites, the representation of the rational world, while the center represents the mystical world. Having Christ in the center reflects that for all human beings to discover their spirituality they have to discover their center, where they will find the door to their own truth. Discovering one's own truth is the main goal of spiritual tradition and discovering its relationship with the universal truth is the main aim of mythology. Campbell also believed that God is a human metaphor as he said, "We keep thinking of deity as a kind of fact, somewhere; God as a fact. God is simply our own notion of something that is symbolic of transcendence and mystery." *{Ref 1, p. 16}*

159

Reference 1. Campbell Joseph (1904-1987) Transformations of Myth Through Time

Perennial Library 1990 Harper and Row Publishers New York USA

Reference 2. Joseph Campbell in Conversation with Michael Toms

Perennial Library Harper and Row Publishers New York USA 1990

Letter No. 31

SPLIT IN OUR PSYCHE

October 8, 2019 at 11:06 PM

Dear Dr. Sohail,

First, thanks for inviting me for a lecture at the gathering of the Family of the Heart group. It was refreshing to find a group that believes in freedom and openness in discussing all relevant topics and perspectives. That is rare and becoming *increasingly* rare in South Asia and in South Asian communities all around the world.

As you suggested, I would summarize my lecture on my view of the split I find in the psyche of the subcontinent, both collectively and individually and its implications as we struggle to bring peace into our personal lives and our South Asian societies. Yes, that would hopefully be useful for our readers also.

But first, a few words on Joseph Campbell and his relevance to my lecture outline below. You summarized very well various aspects of his life and work. I love his assertion that everyone needs to ask themselves, "Where lies my bliss?" To find and engage in work that gives us our bliss, that aligns us with our unique talents, strengths and nature, makes us 'alive'. And that we have to turn inwards for that and no book or teacher outside can give that to us. Krishnamurti would agree.

Campbell also talks about the movement of societies over thousands of years from the goddesses and matriarchy to patriarchal traditions, as you point out. From mythological wisdom that helps us in turning inwards to generic outer ideologies. From inner and inclusive ethics to outer moralities based on black and white, good and bad thinking. Many of these themes are relevant to the history and psyche of the Indo-Pakistan subcontinent.

So, here goes the gist of my lecture…

Internal Conflict in the Psyche of the Subcontinent, both individually and collectively

In Pakistan, and in the subcontinent, we struggle in many ways, collectively and individually, because we carry within us a deep-rooted conflict. We have two sets of roots in our heritage. And it is important to understand them well as they help us realize why we are where we are and more importantly, how we can get out of this place that seems to be suffocating us at present, in Pakistan, India and Bangladesh. And it also shows up in our individual lives, whether we live in the subcontinent or in Canada.

So the first set of roots, more spiritual and heart-based, started with the agricultural and goddess culture of Mehergarh, about 9000 years ago and these roots are very different in nature, as we will show below, to the others. The other set of roots, more patriarchal, formal religions, come from people who migrated to the subcontinent from Central Asia and the West, starting about 3500 years ago. This included their revealed, heavenly, books, the Vedas (and other Sanskrit texts written by the Brahmins) and the Quran (and formal Islamic texts brought in by the Muslim invaders and settlers).

With broad strokes, to outline the essential differences in tendencies, we list some of the characteristics of the two sets of traditions below, so that we can recognize these tendencies and their impact on our individual and collective psyches:

EXPERIENTIAL, HEART-BASED, DEVOTIONAL, SPIRITUAL TRADITIONS	FORMAL, RELIGIOUS TRADITIONS
Indigenous (starting 9000 years ago, or even earlier)	Brought in by outsiders (starting 3500 years ago)
Devi, Temples, Tantra, Yoga, Bhakti, Sufi (there was little to no tradition of writing religious or theological texts, except for poetry)	Vedic, Sanskrit texts (Vedas, Brahmanas, Puranas, Upanisads) and Quran and Sunnah texts (originally no goddesses present in any of these revealed texts)
Earthy – the world was the body of the goddess and spirituality grew out of it	Heavenly – gods living mostly in the skies, and the formal texts were revealed from heavens
Immanent – the divine, the sacred, the spirit is within and can only be reached through the material world	Transcendent – the divine as mostly separate from the material world and mostly in conflict with it (the world is a temptation or a test)
We are part of nature; nature is sacred	Nature is created for us; we need to control nature and human nature
Human body and sexuality are sacred (elevated status of dance; sexuality celebrated in temples and texts; Tantra; Lingam and Yoni at the entrance of many temples)	Human body and sexuality being 'dirty', to be controlled, repressed, covered up (no prayers during menstruation; hijab; dance seen negatively; punishments showing deep fear of sexuality)

Joining hands for Prayers – people would mostly join hands and turn inwards to pray; also to greet others, recognizing the divine in them as well	Opening hands for Prayers – people would mostly open up their hands and look up to the heavens (as in *dua*) to beg for things from above
Darker gods; focus on the moon (more common in the darker local populations)	Focus on sun, light, fairness (more common in the fairer-skinned invaders from colder areas)
Poetry – mostly working with symbols and metaphors *Ilmon bas kareen o yar;* [enough of your sermons, dear friend]	Theological texts – mostly literal, detailed, descriptive texts
Complexity; openness to conflicting realities and ambiguity; creative chaos	Definitions (al-Furqan); clarity; obsessive debates on the right interpretations and definitions
Multiple truth claims	One Truth – focus on oneness (one and *only*)
Coexistence valued; pluralistic in nature; rare examples of the use of violence in converting others to their worldview and values	Tendency and permission to use force or coercion "righteously" in introducing "the right way", the only Truth, to others
Inner ethics – focus on intentions, on the state of the heart *dil darya samundaron doongay, kon dillan dian janey hu;* [Hearts, deeper than rivers and oceans; who knows what lurks therein]	Outer morality – focus on outer behavior and forms (right clothes, how to raise the finger, how to sit, how to pronounce)

Softer in judgment (comfortable with humans being mostly in the grey zone)	Quick to judge (B&W picture, with clearly defined right/wrong, good/bad, virtue/sin, heaven/hell)
Strong in the collective Feminine, Anima	Patriarchal – threatened by body/heart/passion
Fluid	Solid, defined, hierarchical and controlled

The indigenous heart-based spiritual traditions have remained the predominantly *lived* traditions in the subcontinent since thousands of years. They could exist side by side, without having to prove the other wrong or lower than them. So for thousands of years, when we had celebrations in our temple for our goddess, the neighboring villagers would come and celebrate with us and when it was time for their festivals, we would go and celebrate their gods with them.

There was no temple tradition in the original Aryan, Brahman, Sanskrit tradition. Devotion to temples and to Gods and Goddesses was a purely indigenous tendency which developed into a range of Bhakti traditions. When Islam came to the subcontinent, it was the Sufis who were perfectly aligned with this indigenous tendency. This shows up even in the more formal Sufi Orders, as in the Chishtiyya Sufis.

Brahmanism tried to bring all local spiritual traditions under one umbrella, *their* umbrella, assigning a role and position to various tribes and people. The Brahmans, along with the slightly earlier Aryan migrants, the Ksatriyas, ended up being the highest castes, responsible for religion and establishing a rule, in this Dharmic sacred order, and the locals were put in mid- and lower-level, serving castes. In my book, *The Roots of Religious Tolerance in Pakistan and India*, I go into the details of exactly how and when the local groups were lured into, assimilated and subjugated into this hierarchical caste system that defines and limits their lives up to the present day.

The Brahmanic assimilation techniques were aided by two outside factors. The Persians came up with a generic term for the wide range of all the spiritual and religious traditions of the area. The river Sindhu was pronounced as Hindu in old Persian. They called the land to the East of the river, as they were coming over from the West, Hindu Lands. The people were called the Hindu people. The religions and traditions of the lands were called the Hindu religions and Hindu traditions. And Brahmans got the one all-encompassing term that they were looking for.

The second outside help came later from the Europeans. They were also used to revealed religions and had a literary bias towards written texts, much more than lived traditions. So, when they started coming to the subcontinent, to know and document the religious traditions of this region, they started going through the *texts*. Almost all the texts were written by the Brahmans, in Sanskrit, because that is pretty much all they did for thousands of years, all the other work having been assigned to the other castes. The textual bias of the Europeans gave further legitimacy to the Brahmanical Vedic-Sanskrit tradition being the 'backbone' of religions in India. The lived heart-based spiritual traditions continued becoming more and more invisible in the eyes of the world and slowly in the eyes of the local inhabitants as well.

For the present audience, I focused more on the Islamic subjugation of the indigenous psyche. The historical details and examples of this are also documented in my book. But a few examples were enough to bring out the patterns. The subjugation of the local psyche, establishing control and introducing the new patriarchal traditions by the use of force was the modus operandi. Muslim rule was established by destroying and taking over much of what was sacred to life in the subcontinent. Many temples were destroyed. Men, women and children of the conquered towns were often taken as slaves. Women were distributed amongst the commanders and troops according to the religiously permitted *maal-e-ghanimah* (wealth taken by force from the enemy, after winning a war) rules. They could, of course, be raped as and when desired by the appropriate owners. And the lands were plundered in general. From Timur Lung, to Ghaznavi and Ghouri, to various dynasties including the Mughals, there are horrific stories of abuse and plunder of the locals and their traditions.

This description above seems to be harsh and biased. In documenting these details in my book, however, I rely completely on documents recorded by the invaders themselves or by their own historians. Given their inclination towards texts and documentation, some of them kept meticulous daily records in their own journals while most others had historians traveling with them, who saved and documented letters, decrees and accounts of what was being done by these rulers every step of the way. It's just that they did not see anything wrong with documenting what we now see as abuse, through the eyes of human rights and gender sensitivity.

A valid question arises that in history, in almost all areas of the world; various rulers and invaders violated and abused the human rights of local populations. Why, then, should we reflect on ways in which the Muslim invaders of the subcontinent did what they did?

The answer is simple. Because the Muslims of the subcontinent choose to identify themselves with these historical figures, holding them as role models, holding their deeds in high regard, with pride. So much so that the pattern of desecration of the temples of the locals would be seen as an ideal behavior that the Muslims should try emulate. From *butgari* [making of idols] to *butshikani* [idol-breaking], as done by their Muslim ancestors, in the poetry of the poet held in the highest regard, Allama Muhammad Iqbal (RA), for example. So, for example, the act of the destruction of the Shiv temple at Somnat which was revered by about a thousand villages all around it, is described by Iqbal as the ideal that Allah would want the Muslims of the subcontinent to strive towards *{Jawab-i-Shikwa}*.

I often ask groups of Muslims in the subcontinent 'when did we come to the subcontinent?' And the answer is almost always "712 AD". I point out to them that most of us did not come to the subcontinent but have ancestors here going back to 9000 years and more. And that Indian Muslims who had converted to Islam actually *never* ruled the subcontinent. It was never about establishing the Muslim rule but about establishing the Afghans or the Persians or the Arab rule. Otherwise, why would Ibrahim Lodhi fight with Babar or Sher Shah Suri with Humayun and so on and so forth. The rule was never of the Indian Muslims and the distinction was kept very clear in the royal courts. It is only later that Iqbal, needing to raise the self-esteem of the Indian Muslims, introduced the idea of *them* "ruling India". A parallel would be if the local Christians of the subcontinent referred to the British rule as an era where *they* ruled India. It's a rather silly notion but amazingly overlooked by the majority of Muslims whose forefathers at some point converted to Islam giving up on the local traditions.

So, as long as the Muslims of the subcontinent keep identifying with the invaders, keep talking about the destruction of the local traditions and temples with pride, keep gloating over being idol-breakers, keep naming their missiles Ghauri and Ghaznavi, keep saying that *we* did it all, the others can then very justifiably ask them to pay back for it all. And with the Muslim preferred norm of 'an eye for an eye', imagine what that would mean for the Muslim population and the mosques in the subcontinent. Remember 1992... and that was just *one* mosque.

Are the feelings of Muslims for their places of worship somehow more important than the feelings of others for their places of worship? The sooner Muslims start coming out of this myopic vision, the better for them. As the world continues to shrink, *mutual* respect would become the expected norm more and more. Respect only for oneself, demanded with a threat of violence, would be harder and harder to justify.

For a people who regularly refer to Aurangzeb Alamgir as *Rehmatullah-illaih* [may the blessings of Allah be upon him] knowing that he killed his brothers, including the rightful successor, Dara Shikoh (according to their own Mughal rules), imprisoned his father for years, until he became blind and died, how do they justify talking of fairness in governance and democracy? In the same way, for reasons barely hinted at above, how can they talk of gender issues or human rights in the subcontinent?

The traditions or those who migrated to the subcontinent took their toll on the local psyche. However, the roots of the local psyche have been deeper and older and are still alive. Till quite recently we saw these roots still nurturing us and bearing fruit in the form of pluralism and mutual respect in the society. Most mosques did not advertise their loyalty to one or the other sect. When a plate of *halva* [sweets] was sent by some neighbor, no one made an issue of belonging to a sect that does not recognize that day as a day to celebrate. And no one thought much of religion when it came to flying kites, or celebrating harvest or putting henna on the hands or singing songs with a *dholki* [small drum] at the weddings, which all evolved as cultural forms over thousands of years and, if not prescribed in the Quran, are not mentioned in the Vedas or the Gita as well. These are just a few pointers, but all of this becomes relevant as we think of individual and social interventions to make our societies more tolerant, peaceful and pluralistic.

Whether it is the blasting of the Bamyan statues by the Taliban or the three options given by the ISIS to non-Muslims living under their rule, they are all moving back to the more formalistic interpretations of their religion. Most of the cultural celebrations mentioned above have been highly criticized by the Taliban. Where they held power, they banned these practices by force and violence. That included limiting not just the Feminine but making women almost invisible in public spheres. This even included little girls, where thousands of their schools in Pakistan were closed down and many even razed to the ground. The Taliban clearly know what traditions weaken their formalistic, extremist stance. Social activists, wanting to work for peace, just need to pay attention to what the Taliban have done, and do the exact opposite. In that, one of the things the Taliban did all over Pakistan is attack Sufi shrines. We need to take a clue from all they do.

For now, as individuals and as a society, we seem to be sliding farther and farther away from our more pluralistic roots. And the momentum seems to be increasing with every passing day.

I promise not to end the next letter on a bleak note again.

My best regards!

Kamran

Letter No. 32

THE EVOLUTION OF HUMAN CONSCIOUSNESS: FOUR TRADITIONS

October 9, 2019 at 9:18 AM

Dear Kamran,

Your presentation in our Family of the Heart seminar was impressive. It was engaging, inspiring and intellectually stimulating. I am so happy that you were able to capture the essence of your presentation in a few pages. I am sure that our readers would love it as it would make them review their understanding of the struggles of South Asian people and inspire them to build bridges rather than walls between different ethnic and religious communities.

In one of our informal dialogues, I mentioned that Dr. Baland Iqbal and I together produced a series of 35 television programs for Canada One TV titled *"In Search of Wisdom"* that is now saved on YouTube. The idea was to introduce common people to different traditions of the world. The way you captured the essence of your presentation and two distinct traditions, let me try to summarize our programs in four basic traditions that highlight the evolution of human consciousness. Here it is.

~*~

When we reflect on human history and study the evolution of human consciousness, we become aware that throughout history in different communities, countries and cultures, a variety of traditions were created and practiced. There were leaders and followers, there were scholars and philosophers, and there were students and disciples. Rather than going into a detailed academic discussion, I would like to capture the essence of the collective wisdom of the centuries by dividing them into four cultural and philosophical traditions.

The first tradition was the Humanist Tradition. It was presented by Confucius and Lao Tzu in China. Both of these scholars and philosophers presented their ideas and ideals to inspire people to become better human beings individually and collectively. Confucius presented the Golden Rule to humanity and suggested that we need to treat others the way we would like to be treated by them. The Golden Rule became the basis of a caring and compassionate humanist philosophy. Lao Tzu suggested that to lead a simple and meaningful life we need to stay close to nature. He believed that nature's way was Tao and the closer we stay to our own nature and the nature of our environment, the easier it will be for us to lead a healthy, happy and peaceful life.

It is interesting to note that Confucius and Lao Tzu did not mention the concepts of God, prophets, life after death, heaven or hell in their philosophy. They believed that we did not need divine revelations to become better human beings and create just and peaceful communities.

The second tradition was the Spiritual Tradition. It was presented by the Buddha and Mahavira in India. They believed that human attachment to people and possessions is the main source of suffering. Buddha and Mahavira encouraged their followers to learn to meditate and emotionally detach themselves from their environments to find peace. Buddha also believed in a soul separate from the body that kept returning to the earth to purify itself. Once it found enlightenment and nirvana, the soul no longer needed to make this journey.

The third tradition was the Religious Tradition. It was presented by Zarathustra in Iran. Zarathustra presented the ideas of a Heavenly God, Ahura Mazda, the God of Wisdom, divine revelations, sin and virtue, life after death, heaven and hell. Zarathustra believed that if human beings followed divine revelations they would lead a happy and peaceful life on earth and go to heaven in the afterlife.

Zarathustra's ideas and ideals became popular in the Middle East and became part of Abrahamic religious traditions that gave birth to Judaism, Christianity and Islam. Those three monotheistic religions are the offspring of Zarathustrian ideology. Their followers also believe in a soul separate from the body; but such a soul does not come back to earth like the Buddhist soul, rather it waits for the Day of Judgment to be sent to hell or heaven. Since the followers of Christianity and Islam believed in preaching, their preachers traveled to the four corners of the world to spread the holy message. Some followers of these religions also believed in holy wars--crusades and jihads. Because of those preachers and holy warriors there are billions of followers of Christianity and Islam all over the world.

The fourth tradition was the Philosophical Tradition. It was presented by Greek philosophers like Hippocrates, Socrates, Plato and Aristotle. These philosophers presented the idea that all things and events in life follow the laws of nature and by knowing those laws we can unravel the mysteries of nature.

Hippocrates became the Father of Medicine. He told his patients that rather than praying and fasting and offering sacrifices to Gods for their sins, they should heal their bodies by a balanced diet, a good night's sleep, and regular exercise. He believed that walking was the best exercise. Hippocrates was the first physician who separated medicine from religion.

Socrates, another Greek philosopher, became the Father of Philosophy. He encouraged logical, rational and analytical thinking as he believed that reason was more important than revelation to solve human problems. Socrates inspired young people to question and challenge age-old traditions. Many traditional Greeks did not like the Socratic Method, so they accused him of misguiding the youth and not believing in the Greek gods. As his punishment, Socrates was forced to drink a cup of poison and sacrifice his life for his ideals. Socrates did not write down his ideas and ideals but his student Plato documented his philosophy in the form of dialogues, because Socrates believed that dialogue, rather than a monologue, was a better way to discover the truth. He believed that an unexamined life was not worth living.

Plato created an academy to teach philosophy and science that became the prototype of modern Western universities. Plato's student Aristotle made valuable contributions to the world of politics. Greek philosophers offered a road map to create a just and peaceful republic. They also made significant contributions to the disciplines of science and human psychology.

Over the centuries, Greek philosophers were translated and introduced to Europe by Arab philosophers like Al Kindi, Al Farabi, Avicenna and Ibn Rushd. Based on the foundations laid down by Greek philosophers, European scholars built tall buildings of philosophy and science.

In the last three centuries, sciences and disciplines employing scientific thinking came up with significant developments that revolutionized our thinking. Examples, of those who contributed would include biologists like Charles Darwin, psychologists like Sigmund Freud, sociologists like Karl Marx and cosmologists like Steven Hawking.

While scientists were discovering methods to collect evidence and discover the laws of nature, caring and compassionate reformers from different communities and cultures were discovering ways to resolve conflicts gracefully. They presented their secular ideas and humanist ideals and fought for human rights. These philosophers and reformers like Leo Tolstoy, Mohandas Gandhi and Martin Luther King, Jr. inspired their followers to rise above racial, religious, linguistic and gender differences and discover common bonds of humanity. They shared with us that to create a peaceful world we need to cherish our differences and recognize that we are all part of the same family, the human family.

In the contemporary world, peaceful followers of different religious and spiritual, secular and scientific traditions are breaking down walls of ignorance and prejudice and building bridges of caring and compassion, harmony and peace so that we can all grow to the next stage of human evolution, become fully human, and create a peaceful world together. These are our dreams but we need to dream before we can make them realities.

Dear Kamran,

Why don't we conclude our book by offering some suggestions to our readers that might inspire them to become part of the peace movement? Can you share your suggestions and strategies that would help our readers to become peaceful human beings individually and collectively? Maybe you can focus on Pakistan and I can review Nobel Peace Prize lectures and share a summary.

What do you think?

Peacefully yours,

Sohail

Letter No. 33

DIRECT STRATEGIES FOR PEACE

October 10, 2019 at 10:38 PM

Dear Dr. Sohail,

Thanks for sharing your classification of the evolution of human consciousness. I find your ability to categorize things very helpful in seeing the different kinds of developments and evolutions. The examples you give in each category help me understand that group better. I see many parallel developments within each category. But the flow of ideas within each category, currents going from one to the other part of the world, is truly amazing. The beginnings of the spiritual developments one could take even before Buddhism and Jainism perhaps, and have other parallel developments in other parts of the world. I absolutely love that you take the beginnings of Humanism back to Lao Tzu and Confucius. It makes perfect sense given how we define Humanism.

At the end of your letter, you asked me to start thinking of strategies for peace. During all of my philosophical explorations and venturing out into the mystical realms, this was my one continuing quest: an exploration of possible interventions into extremism. I see this in the letters I have written to you as well. I now wish I had, in my mind, in my life, at least framed it more as "exploring initiatives for peace" instead of "interventions into extremism and militancy". My energies remained focused on eliminating the negative instead of expanding the positive. *Thinking* of how to fight the negative instead of *living* and *being* the positive. I say this because I have lately started noticing this, not just in myself, but in many of our peace activists and social activist friends as well. While it seems like a subtle shift, it may make all the difference. I will come back to this in a while. But, this is what I appreciate in my sister

Fouzia Saeed, who has been a tremendous activist, but from a place of celebrating the cultural and creative life. And that, Dr. Sohail, is what I find most refreshing in you as well. The positivity. Being at peace within. The joy of being alive. And this "living", while being a powerful intervention, is lived not as a means to an end but as an end in itself. It is a pleasure to see this, even though I myself am not there yet. So, in this also, there is a part of me that tracks the coordinates provided by you, wants to keep checking my internal GPS and feels that if I keep moving, I should get there too. And then there is the other, observing self, that reminds me that it is not about getting to some other place but being where I am. And a third that stands aside and looks at both, laughing out loud. I know. Enough of this!

OK, so interventions or initiatives for peace... In the interest of space and time, let me very briefly say just a few lines for each strategic area that stands out for me. I will go from the more concrete and direct to the more indirect and deeper ones. The direct ones are more obvious but they almost always also bring up more resistance and strong reactions from the extremists. The indirect ones are slower changes that address the causes more and would produce longer lasting results. Both levels can be worked on simultaneously. To protect the tree, one sprays the leaves and the fruits that are already there at present, in addition to treating the roots, for all the future seasons to come as well.

The extremist narrative and the formalistic roots that nurture it, that protect it, that divert our attention to other things, are being bombarded at us from all directions today. This bombardment needs to stop. In reality, it remains unchecked, for the most part.

Some of us feel afraid to challenge the extremist narrative. Some, because we feel afraid to challenge it, tell ourselves that "what's so wrong with it after all". This is a version of an individual and collective "Stockholm syndrome". With time we buy in, accept and justify something that if we were to challenge, we are afraid could threaten our lives. The fear of violence holds us hostage and keeps us from breaking free, from thinking of breaking free, collectively and individually.

For more than a year I used to do a 10-minute segment for a TV channel on youth issues. I would squeeze in Bulleh Shah or some pluralistic ideas every now and then, that would challenge the formalistic religious mindset. So, the producer of the program would often tell me that "please do not bring in religion because we are not supposed to be talking about religion". Which I would tell him was a complete lie. In the very same program, they had so many weekly segments on formalistic topics. One even on Quranic therapy. On what to recite how many times for which psychological or physical ailment, blowing on water, and all. The truth is that they have no problem showing what is pleasing to the formalistic and violent side but cannot risk showing the other side, lest they offend the violent ones.

A female friend of mine said to me how much she feels offended, as a woman, with horrible displays of oppressive and repressive clothing. Many progressive people feel hurt by discrimination and violence coming from formalism. But they just choose to not get violent every time they feel offended or hurt. They don't block roads and start burning random motorcycles, hurling stones and killing bystanders while they are at it. But no one is willing to say to those showing formalistic outbursts, 'while you may be hurt, *this* does not make much sense... *at all!*'

Realistically, even if most of us would not dare to, or want to, challenge the extremist, or the much more pervasive, formalistic narrative, we can still do much to limit our exposure to it. And that of our family and friends, whatever circle of influence we have. Limiting our exposure to televangelists. Being very conscious of what we watch. Trimming our social media lists and subscriptions. Setting healthy boundaries and building healthy support networks (like what you have created here with the Family of the Heart). Otherwise, the formalistic rhetoric and worldview have an invasive tendency built into it to creep in. That, the creeping in of formalism, is the reality of what is happening to individuals and families all over the country today.

On a more Institutional level, it would make sense to demand, and to keep pushing certain institutions to do their job, to keep public discourse free from inciting violence and murder at least. This goes from Friday sermons to video statements on social media. Once violence explodes, when it happens in the name of religion, every now and then we see some action taken against those who are braking, burning and killing. But much more of that needs to happen. Illegal is illegal. A crime is a crime. And that should mean something.

There is a commonly held belief that the military had been feeding extremist narratives at different times in the history of the country, to create "freedom fighters" and the "good Taliban". Because the military remains beyond the audit or legal systems of the country, any such interventions from them have unclear and long-lasting impact. Demanding at least more transparency in the tactics employed by them would always be in the better interest of the country, as the citizens of the country eventually have to live with the consequences of the decisions made by the military, no matter how well-intentioned they may be.

While enough has been said and done about it, the textbook reforms and the education reforms, in general, remains an area that we are actually sliding backward in. Any positive changes in making the textbooks less hateful or discriminatory were met with extreme reactions. And everyone backs off again. And on any hopes that were there to get a handle on the Madrassa situation, it seems clear that we are not going to go far in that direction either. Mainstreaming madrassas, it seems, no longer means changing their curriculum much but allowing them to issue even Masters level degrees. If that happens, that will bring their graduates into regular jobs in most of the mainstream government and private institutions. And that will go far in mainstreaming their narrative in the country. We might as well close down the parallel Government school system. So, while we actually seem to be sliding backward on that front, any pressure, direct or indirect, on the relevant institutions to counter these trends would be helpful.

In line with my lecture to the Family of the Heart, that I summarized recently, if we were ever at that point where this could happen, it would be very important to have in-depth, popular reflections on our role models, on the actual history of invaders who also happened to be Muslims, on the crimes committed against the people of the subcontinent, on institutionalized discrimination and violence, on the historically realistic identity of the pre-partition Indian Muslims, on the modern relations and boundaries between religious and national identities etc. Given our deep national identity confusion and insecurity on certain issues, this would be very difficult for Pakistanis to achieve. This, however, is a necessary individuation and maturation process and its impact could go far in allowing Pakistan to emerge as a modern nation-state in the world today.

Also discussed, in the lecture mentioned above, was the comfort level that our indigenous psyche had with loosely defined identities. Outside of the formal traditions, people in South Asia were used to having multiple identities that they easily moved in and out of. As an example, I had mentioned how about 30% of Gorakhnathi Jogis in the Jhelum Gazetteer, belonging to a left-handed Saiva tradition, counted themselves as Muslims as well. With the current rise of the formal psyche, we see rigidity in the religious identities where this would not even be imaginable today. Could an area of indirect intervention be to reinforce and strengthen parallel identities that soften the reliance on the more rigid religious ones? For example, if an increasing number of Pakistanis identify most strongly with their one religious identity, why not let them have ownership and pride in other non-Islamic or Pre-Islamic identities.

To give just one example, helping people to have some pride in owning one of the earliest human civilizations, Mehergarh. Bollywood produced a movie "*Mohenjo Daro*" with top cast, on the ancient *Indian* civilization. While most Pakistanis repeat the mindless mantra, "we came to the subcontinent in 712 AD." I brought it up in a group in Pakistan once and someone very intelligently explained to me that at *that* time it was all India. Neither India nor Pakistan was a name that existed 4500 years ago. Certainly not 9000 years ago. Names keep changing. Egypt was not the name of the country when the ancient 'Egyptian' civilization flourished there. But it's called after whatever country owns the area now. So, Mohenjo Daro and Mehergarh are ancient *Pakistani* civilizations. I find it so sad that we are not willing to own what could be a source of pride for us. So... in line with the strategy of strengthening parallel identities, an intervention could be to strengthen our Indus Valley or Gandhara identities. Starting, in Taxila, an Institute for the Study of South Asian Cultures and Traditions, for example.

And now for the big one, that also was discussed some in my lecture and its summary. An obvious way to counter the formalistic streak in our psyche would be to nurture our much older and much deeper roots in the more spiritual part of our heritage. On the surface, this means balancing the increasingly rigid and formalistic Islam with the more pluralistic and tolerant Sufism. Much has been written in support of this by many. We cannot get into details here, but grant me the luxury to say a bit more than a few lines on this one. We need to be rather careful in going this route.

One dominant view is that we can rely on the Sufi Wisdom to come up with deeper and spiritual interpretations of the formal Islamic texts, including the Quran. A very similar notion is to come up with scientific interpretations to bring more rationality into the more conservative and rigid understanding of the formal texts. In either case, in addition to the obvious benefit of broadening the perspective, we are also reinforcing for people that, whether they deal with this or that interpretation, the ultimate authority lies with the formal texts. So, we may help them shift to a deeper perspective but at the same time, we make them more dependent on outside texts and teachers for knowing the truth. The basic notion of turning inwards, of waking up to the power within, is lost. I am reminded of Krishnamurti again. But if a better interpretation is all one is hoping for, then this works. *I* have started to resist the temptation to go this route.

One of my concerns in giving more power to formal religious writings, ideas and symbols, even when we are bringing out their most spiritual meaning and understanding, is that as people get even more deeply entrenched and attached to these religious symbols, anyone can abuse this attachment and the passion that it results in, to bring about more polarization and fragmentation in the people. One thinks that Sufi and Bhakti traditions would open our hearts and increase empathy. But when religious or even spiritual devotion to a symbol or idea exists without the overall pluralistic mindset, where we had *mutual* respect for the passionate faith of others as well, the resulting devotion to the one truth can be explosive. Remember that the Babri Mosque was destroyed by Ram *bhakts* [passionate devotees]. I know there were politicians behind it, who were using the passion of the *bhakts* for their political purposes, but I do believe the people who came out in the streets, *were* responding to the passion of devotion to their god. The problem is that, for thousands of years, devotion brought softness to our hearts because it was part of a system where it was tempered with pluralism and respect for multiple truths, coexisting truths. Most of the death and destruction in

Pakistan that has been unleashed, repeatedly, in relation to the blasphemy laws and their abuse was *led*, not by the Taliban, but by those who consider themselves the followers of the Sufis, by Ahl-e-Sunnah Wal Jamaat. And the first revivalist movement of Islam in the subcontinent, the most rigid interpretation of Islam, came out of the Sufi order of the Naqshbandiyya. So, I tell my activist friends interested in Sufism, *be wary*!

There is another notion of accepting things the way they are, of *tawakkul*, of fate, of destiny, in Sufism, that is of concern. These notions and the resulting attitudes can easily serve to maintain the status quo. They can easily be abused by those who want to rule people and who do not want them to question or challenge the way things are. One can write so much about the deeper meaning of these concepts in Sufi *tareeqat*, but I just wanted to flag it as a potential danger here. Using Sufism for psychological or social interventions has to be done very carefully and with a deeper understanding of what could easily become serious pitfalls.

Then there is the problem of the power that is given to the Sufi teachers on the Sufi path, and I have already shared my experiences with that and the rampant abuse of that power that we all know about. The scene at the Sufi shrines today, in spite of all the benefits, is a minefield, with many underlying, not-so-obvious dangers, buried all over the place.

However, after cautioning people of the abuse at the shrines and of using Sufism in general, I do still end up using Sufi *Poetry* of the old Sufi poets quite often. That poetry still speaks to people in a very deep way and has the power to open them up very powerfully. Heterodox Sufis, like Bulleh Shah, were not afraid to shatter all the hypocrisy inherent in the formal religious structures and free us from orthodox religion and spirituality.

Dear Dr. Sohail, I told myself that I would only write a few lines for each area of intervention and then I cannot help but clarify some of the areas a little more, even while summarizing them. There is so much to say. And I leave so much out. But let me take a break here. In my next letter, I would write to you about some of the more indirect strategies that, in my experience, can be equally effective and significant.

My best regards for now.

Kamran

Letter No. 34

INDIRECT AND LONG-TERM STRATEGIES FOR PEACE

October 12, 2019 at 11:17 AM

Dear Dr. Sohail,

I hope you are doing well. My mind has been rolling ever since I stopped with only the direct strategies for peace. This is because with time I have found that the indirect strategies for peace can be as effective in the short run and, in addition, can have a longer lasting impact. I find them much closer to my heart today.

At the end of my letter, I was talking of Sufism. There I mentioned the whole concept of the surrender of intellect. I was talking to Dr. Pervez Hoodbhoy once and, from what I can recollect, one of his core interventions for countering excessive religiosity was to increase the student's, and indeed everyone's, ability to question, to think critically and analyze things rationally and logically.

The wife of a very good friend of mine had both the military and Al-Huda in the environment that she grew up in. Her son, a very intelligent young man, was once visiting us along with her. He was playing upstairs with other kids while she was sitting at the dining table with us. When she felt it was time to go, she called him loudly to leave. He said, "Why do we have to go so early, mama?" Her response was fascinating to me. First, she had him come down. Then in front of my parents and all, she asked him why he should not be asking questions? Embarrassed, he pleaded that it was OK and that he was ready to go. But, no. She said, "Answer me, why should we not question?" He said, in a tone that told me he had done this many times before also, "because Allah does not like people who question?" My jaw dropped.

This notion that one should not question *in general,* period, is not uncommon, unfortunately. It is coupled with the notion that there are some things about religion that should not be thought too deeply about and that if you do that you would go crazy!

What is critical to introduce, in whatever way possible, is Epistemology, questioning how we know what we know, how we check the validity and reliability of an idea, along with basic ability to question and think logically and rationally.

What I often find in people who are *rigidly* and intolerantly following their one truth is that they have not had the opportunity to expose themselves to the wide range of perspectives, priorities and belief systems in the world. Or they have the opportunity but not the will to do so. The more insecure they are, the narrower the focus of their blinders to any other belief systems outside of their own. In my assessment, being deeply aware of other perspectives is very helpful in increasing our tolerance levels and mutual understanding and respect. And if possible, actual interactions with people who hold different perspectives can be the most powerful way to build sensitivity, as long as the interactions happen in a mutually respectful place with equality and openness.

In terms of interventions, this means allowing people to have more exposure to literature, movies and whenever possible, with actual people from other cultures and beliefs. There are so many books and movies that one wish were translated or dubbed into Urdu and regional languages in Pakistan. There are publishing houses that have played this role and one feels grateful to them. We need much more of this though.

Dear Dr. Sohail, this is again where one appreciates you so much. In what you have produced, you are constantly opening up new and broader perspectives, new ways of looking at life and of living life. And not just your own ideas, but you keep introducing people to the wide range of writers and philosophers and scholars and *their* ideas and perspectives as well. The fact that you are able to do this in Urdu is of critical importance to make it all accessible to more and more people in Pakistan. In less than a month of having known you, I have heard of so many people who are regularly following your columns and books and treat you with... "reverence" is the word that comes to mind.

Creativity is one of the most significant factors. Art, music, dance, poetry, literature, theater, cinema and many other forms of creativity have the power to touch, move and bring the heart to life. They often come out of the heart and touch the heart. And it's the fluid heart traditions that can counter, or at least balance, the rigidity of the formal traditions.

In this, I respect the work of my sister Fouzia, who has worked to preserve and popularize creative cultural expressions in Pakistan, in all of their forms. That becomes a soft intervention that is much deeper and much more effective in bringing some moisture to our increasingly dry and rigid psyche.

What Fouzia also points out is that along with creating whatever creative spaces we can, we need to consciously and proactively protect the progressive spaces that have been part of our ancient heritage and that are shrinking at an alarming rate. The conservative forces have been very strategic in this. Khuda Hafiz was changed to Allah Hafiz, from the protection of God (in general) to the protection of the one Muslim God, Allah, thereby excluding minorities. It became OK for complete strangers to tell women to cover their heads. Attack a shrine here. Kill a *Qawwal* there. Some bloggers disappear. A Vice-Chancellor of a University gets killed for allowing a music concert. A student gets lynched. And slowly everyone starts to watch what they say and what they do, out of fear. Shrinking progressive spaces. And that has to be challenged on all levels.

During the Taliban times, Dr. Sohail, I was in and out of Afghanistan every few months, though more for psychological work. All of the creative forms mentioned above were not just discouraged but *banned* by the Taliban. So, in the group and even more so in individual sessions, I was listening to horror stories all the time. The Vice and Virtue teams would roam around in their pick-up trucks. Cars would be stopped randomly and checked and if there was a cassette player in it, it would be broken along with all the cassettes. And the owner of the car punished, of course. I remember listening to Rumi being sung with musical instruments playing in the basement, but secretly, with the constant fear of any sound going out and inviting the wrath of the Vice and Virtue police.

During the Taliban years, it was not just creativity, but aesthetics and beauty also that were made invisible, as much as they could. Men would not be allowed to even trim their beards, or they would be put in prison for 6 days. And women, of course, were not to be seen. So many of them related painful stories of getting beaten up with sticks because a bit of the forearm was showing or for wearing the wrong kind of provocative socks on their feet. Hands and feet are all that showed, of course.

Beauty and aesthetics move the heart and make it softer, catching a clue from why the Taliban would ban it. Beauty kills the beast within. So, from creating beauty to preserving and appreciating it, there is a wide range of personal and social interventions that I would not go into the details of here.

Wanting women to disappear from the public eye, pushing them into *burqas*, *hijabs* or ideally in the four walls of their homes, goes much deeper than the repression of aesthetics and beauty. It is the threat that, not just the women, but the collective "Feminine" poses to the dry, rigid, formal psyche. Women have to come out more. And the Feminine has to come out more, in both women *and* men. This again relates to the creative side talked about above.

But, yes, wanting not to see women also has to do with sexuality, of course. And that is a huge area of divergence between the pluralistic body-based traditions and the intolerant, formalistic, heavenly traditions. The fear of sexuality in formal religions is tremendous. And the level of unhealthiness around sexuality in our society, requires a separate book. A series of books. Here I just want to say that anything we can do to bring relatively healthier expressions of sexuality into our personal and societal lives would be helpful.

In one of my TV interviews, one observation I made, that many people repeated to me years later also, had to do with the fact that I can slap my wife in public and no one would say anything. Even the police would say that it's a *nijji muamila* [a domestic issue]. But if I were to kiss her in public, my own wife, then I am spreading immorality and would be picked up immediately. We are fine with public displays of violence but not of love. In Pakistan, Dr. Sohail, 'Make love not war' gets reversed. We give medals and sing songs to honor those who kill the most in wars while walking around, pretending to be asexual beings. And so of course sexuality shows up in the most inappropriate places, in the most grotesque forms.

And in talking of the heart traditions, where do we begin to talk of love. In that, Dr. Sohail, what I often tell people who I find are serious in working for peace in the society, is to read up on the Lover Archetype. The Lover-within knows. So, to bring as much of that into their lives and their work as possible. There is then the traditional folklore around lovers that is very deep in our psyche and something to stay connected with and worked with, in a hundred different creative ways.

Going deeper... we come to the power of humanizing experiences. In *The Root of Religious Tolerance*, I wrote:

"The psyche of the subcontinent, it appears, is familiar with a level of existence that is much more immediate and much closer to our basic humanness than anything that can be captured in religious or spiritual discourse. It is recognized on this level that there can be many truth-claims in reality and the reality of life is always more than what any one truth or any one religious or social or moral system can encompass."

There was a woman, Ayesha, who joined a volunteer training at Bedari Crisis Center that I just did not like as much, right from the beginning. In the very first session of the training, she had mentioned her parents having a servant who was apparently being physically abused by her husband. She mentioned in passing that this servant was working in the kitchen of her mother and had not told anyone that she was a Christian. Once she was caught in a tight spot where she had to pray and Ayesha realized that she did not know how to pray properly. Once exposed, the woman quietly disappeared at night, never to be seen again. After the session, I asked Ayesha about her servant. She said it's not that she was not a Muslim, but that she lied about it. "If she had told us the truth, we may still have given her the job. She did confirm, when I inquired, that her mother had never had a Christian in her kitchen. It was the righteous arrogance in her, with a total lack of awareness of her discrimination that irritated me about her. I was generally hesitant to have volunteers working in the program who had strong biases or discriminatory behaviors. But somehow I kept her in the training while keeping an eye on her.

One of the women that Ayesha worked closely with during the following months was Sonia, who needed support with a whole range of services. At the Center, I only supervised the psychological support which was provided only by a few female psychologists. The groups of volunteers we trained every six months, supported the women coming in for psychological support, in all kinds of other areas. So, Ayesha accompanied Sonia in her visits to the police station, to the lawyer and then to the court. And then she saw Sonia facing security threats and finally drove her to the Government shelter, along with Sonia's five-year-old daughter. Once, after she came back from the shelter, where she had taken some food for Sonia and her daughter, she asked for a debriefing session with me. She talked about all that Sonia was telling her, while they had lunch together, and all the ways in which Sonia had suffered. And Ayesha cried and cried.

I knew that Ayesha knew that Sonia was Christian but the power of the human connection, of the shared experiences, was so strong that it broke through all surface ideological boundaries and allowed them to connect on a level much more basic, much more human. The question of whether Sonia was Christian or not was so irrelevant at this level. I have seen young people who volunteered to work at an orphanage go through similar transitions where the immediacy of the human connection takes them to a place where whether a particular child is Christian or Muslim or Hindu loses all its meaning. That is the power of direct, deep human connections and humanizing experiences.

Dear Dr. Sohail, this letter keeps getting longer and I find it hard to stop. But, there is just one more thing that I must add. It's what I had written to you in an earlier letter as well.

I recognize that these interventions cannot be just a mind-game. That they need to come from the right place. A place of integration and of *being*. Let me quote a few lines from my own writing, 20 years ago. The list of interventions was much shorter then but this is what wrote at the end of it:

"I am talking about these interventions in a very objective and clinical manner. But all the while I know that being a part of the system, I carry within myself the seeds of all the growing problems that I see in the psyche of the subcontinent, including the dryness, the rigidity, the fragmentation of the spirit. Any mechanical intervention from where I stand right now is likely to fail. The journey starts with our own inner healing. Or at least it goes in step with it. However, I also know that the strengths of the collective pluralistic psyche, the spirit of Heer-Ranjha, also lie, even if dormant, deep within our psyche. It is on an individual and collective level that we need to invoke the powers of these archetypes. Only from a place of integration and deeper connectedness can healing flow."

And it rings truer today than it did 20 years ago. Which does not say much for my work, inside or out, during these last two decades.

So, Dr. Sohail, I have done spirituality and I have done psychotherapy and I have done social activism out there, but I still feel the gap, the lack of integration within. Not just that, but the gap seems to be widening and deepening. And in that, I keep pace with the land that I come from. The only difference is that I see and feel the gap more clearly and more vividly now than I did 20 years ago. I wish I could nicely wrap this letter up. I wish I had a clear conclusion. But there it is... a gap, a chasm, an open wound. Inside and out.

You asked me to share my suggestions and strategies that would help our reader to become peaceful human beings, individually and collectively. I have pointed to some strategies. But I have primarily shared what I have gone through and what I still struggle with myself, on this journey. And from that, the readers can extract lessons for themselves, depending on where they are right now in their own journeys. Are there any *ultimate* answers? There are certainly some answers one comes across along the way. But to me, the journey itself seems significant and meaningful. The journey into our own depths, into our inner wisdom and into our lives intensely lived, with peace and harmony.

So, is this a happy or a gloomy note for me to end on? I distinctly remember writing to you that I would not end on a gloomy note again. But as the Sufis would say, the truth of where I am, my *Haq*, above all. Honored by your generosity, openness and integrity, I would not dream of giving you anything less.

I do request you to share your wisdom on the movements to achieve peace on a global level.

With much love and gratefulness!

Kamran

Letter No. 35

PEACE MAKERS

October 14, 2019 at 21:48 PM

Dear Kamran,

After reading your two letters all I can say is WOW. And I have a new interpretation of WOW that you might like:

Words Of Wisdom.

Thanks for sharing your knowledge, experience and wisdom. Your heart is a gold mine and I am so glad your creative juices are flowing in these letters. They are flowing so naturally and spontaneously and creatively that you have a hard time making them stop.

Dear Kamran, I am so impressed by your dedication and commitment to promoting peace in the subcontinent. But I feel that you have been hard on yourself. You judge yourself harshly. You have done more for peace than any other psychologist, psychiatrist, psychotherapist and social activist that I know personally. That is why I was inspired to invite you for a lecture in our FOTH seminar and also inspired to create a book with you in the form of letters.

Dear Kamran,

While your experiences are more practical, pragmatic and hands-on, my encounters are more academic and theoretical and with books of ideas and ideals. One of these days I will present you my two books, *"Prophets of Violence, Prophets of Peace"* and *"From Holy War to Global Peace"* to read and reflect on.

After doing 35 television episodes on *"In Search of Wisdom"*, these days Dr. Baland Iqbal and I are recording another series titled *"In Search of Peace"*. For that series I am reviewing Nobel Peace Prize Lectures. I have written an essay that captures the summary and essay of those lectures. These ideas complement the ideas you have shared in the last two letters.

PEACE MAKERS

While in every community, country and culture there are people who have violent consciousness and create conflict and war, there are others who promote harmony and peace. Some of them create peace in their families, schools and local communities, while others create peace at a national and international level as they want to be part of creating a peaceful world together.

To create peace on earth we need to decrease all those factors that contribute towards creating violence, conflict and war and increase all those factors that help in resolving conflicts peacefully. We are all aware that, like health is more than the absence of illness, peace is also more than the absence of war, at a local, national and international level.

To have a better understanding of the dynamics of peace I have been studying Nobel Peace Lectures for the last few years. During that study, I became acutely aware that peace is like a rainbow that has many colors and each color is a significant component of creating a peace rainbow. Let me share a few colors of that peace rainbow.

ECONOMIC PEACE

Those communities and countries where there is a wide gap between the rich and the poor, the 'haves' and the 'have-nots', are quite vulnerable to an outbreak of violence. Those who live in huts and see their children go to bed hungry while their neighbors live in palaces, become angry with an uneven distribution of wealth and resources. Those who are deprived of the basic necessities of life – food, shelter, education, health care and work, start losing hope, self-respect and dignity. They become so frustrated that finally they become desperate and violent and want to destroy the system that has not served them well. They want a social, economic and political system that will provide them safety and security, justice and peace.

There are many economists, sociologists and socialists who believe that economic conditions are intimately connected with peace. To create a peaceful world we need to fight poverty. Mohammad Yunus from Bangladesh is one of those wise people who has been fighting poverty and hunger and has been quite successful. That is why he was awarded the Nobel Peace Prize in 2006. In his Peace Lecture he shared that after discussing world-renowned economic theories in the university academic circles, he realized that poverty needs to be fought in the streets and huts rather than in the lecture halls. He started the Grameen Bank, a Village Bank, in Bangladesh and arranged small loans for women to start small businesses. Over the years the bank expanded and more and more women took loans to raise their standard of living above the poverty line. At the time of the Nobel Lecture, there were nearly seven million women, from 73,000 villages, who had benefited by that bank. Helping seven million women had helped seven million families in Bangladesh.

Mohammad Yunus believed that since *"poverty is a threat to peace"*, fighting poverty will pave the way for peaceful living and create peaceful communities and countries. Yunus also helped many beggars to start their own businesses and lead a respectful and meaningful life.

Yunus believes that globalization is a mixed blessing. On the one hand, it connects different parts of the world, but on the other hand, it helps Multinational Companies to prosper and progress making it very difficult for small companies and businesses to thrive. He compares globalization with a global highway with one hundred lanes. On that highway, big trucks and vans survive while small rickshaws are pushed away in the ditch of desperation. He suggests that economic progress needs to be linked with social progress so that when big companies and organizations succeed, they are required to share their wealth and profit with the poor people and help them become successful, so that the gap between the rich and the poor decreases and we create a more just and balanced world. Yunus highlights that, "Poverty is not created by the poor people". It is rather created by the policies of rich people that serve a minority rather than the majority. Over the years, Yunus's concept of the Grameen Bank has been adopted by many poor and developing countries.

SOCIAL PEACE

Alongside economic peace, we also need social peace. To create social peace, people from different ethnic, racial, religious and cultural backgrounds have to get along and learn to resolve their conflicts peacefully. Such an environment is created when the state has laws that respect human rights, people have developed a social consciousness and a humanist attitude, and communities have risen above the tribal mentality.

One of the leaders of the 20th- century who fought for social peace was Martin Luther King, Jr. who received the Nobel Peace Prize in 1964 for his involvement in the Civil Rights Movement, a movement that took a new turn in America when an older Black woman, Rosa Parks, would not offer her seat in the bus to a young White man. The movement escalated when Blacks went on strike and boycotted buses and walked to work. That was the time when Martin Luther King, Jr. made passionate speeches until the unjust law was changed. He believed that "it is better to suffer in dignity than to accept segregation in humiliation."

In his Nobel Lecture, King highlighted that Blacks in America have been suffering for a long time because of the color of their skin. He wanted that injustice to end so that Blacks could live with dignity and self-respect. He believed that "oppressed people cannot remain oppressed forever."

King was against relying on violence as he was a peaceful leader and wanted to accomplish peaceful goals with peaceful means. He did not believe, like many leaders of his time, that the end justifies the means. He shared his philosophy about the psychology of violence in these words:

"Violence as a way of achieving racial justice is both impractical and immoral. I am not unmindful of the fact that violence often brings about momentary results. Nations have frequently won their independence in battle. But in spite of temporary victories, violence never brings permanent peace. It solves no social problem: it merely creates new and more complicated ones. Violence is impractical because it is a descending spiral ending in destruction for all. It is immoral because it seeks to humiliate the opponent rather than win his understanding: it seeks to annihilate rather than convert. Violence is immoral because it thrives on hatred rather than love. It destroys the community and makes brotherhood impossible. It leaves society in monologue rather than dialogue. Violence ends up defeating itself. It creates bitterness in the survivors and brutality in the destroyers."

King and his followers were willing to sacrifice, even offer their lives, for their ideals but were not willing to take the lives of others. King was a follower of Mohandas Gandhi, the prophet of non-violence, who was a disciple of Leo Tolstoy, a prophet of peace. Followers of the Tolstoy-Gandhi-King tradition of the 20th century strived to create a peaceful world by peaceful means. They promoted human rights for all races.

HUMAN RIGHTS AND PEACE

In the 20th century, the social consciousness of the whole of humanity reached a level that created the Universal Declaration of Human Rights. Such a declaration offered a promise that all human beings, irrespective of their race or religion, ethnicity or gender, sexual orientation or language, would be treated equally by their countries, communities and cultures. It was a major breakthrough in the human rights and peace movements. Unfortunately, those ideals have not become a ground reality in many parts of the world. But at least people have the ideals to strive and struggle for. Millions of people all over the world are still suffering but human rights activists are fighting for their cause. One of them is Shirin Ebadi, the first Muslim woman who was given the Nobel Peace Prize in 2003. She shared in her Nobel Lecture, "Unfortunately, however, this year's report by the United Nations Development Program (UNDP), as in the previous years, spells out the rise of a disaster that distances mankind from the idealistic world of the authors of the Universal Declaration of Human Rights. In 2002, almost 1.2 billion human beings lived in glaring poverty, earning less than one dollar a day." Ebadi from Iran, like Mohammad Yunus from Bangladesh, strongly feels that poverty is a grave threat to human rights and world peace.

Ebadi feels strongly that while millions of poor and desperate people are suffering in the poor countries of the third world, the rich and the affluent of the first world are becoming insensitive to their needs and are making policies that deprive others of their basic human rights. Governments of the first world do not respect the human rights of the people of the third world. One such example is the large number of prisoners of the war on terror. She said, "...hundreds of individuals who were arrested in the course of military conflicts have been imprisoned in Guantanamo, without the benefit of the rights stipulated under the International Geneva conventions, the Universal Declaration of Human Rights and the [United Nations] International Covenant on Civil and Political Rights." These practices make it very clear that the American Government does not practice what it preaches in the whole world.

Harold Pinter, the British playwright, winner of the Nobel Award of Literature, in his Nobel Lecture challenges the international community with these words, "What has happened to our moral sensibility? Did we ever have any? What do these words mean? Do they refer to a term very rarely employed these days....conscience? A conscience has to do not only with our own acts but to do with our shared responsibility in the acts of others? Is all this dead? Look at Guantanamo Bay. Hundreds of people detained without charge for over three years, with no legal representation or due process, technically detained forever. This totally illegitimate structure is maintained in defiance of the Geneva Convention. It is not only tolerated but hardly thought about by what's called the "international community."

Harold Pinter was very critical of American foreign policy that not only undermines human rights but also threatens world peace. He highlights the character of America's relationship with other countries in the last few decades in these words, "Direct invasion of a sovereign state has never in fact been America's favored method. In the main, it has preferred what it has described as "low-intensity conflict". Low-intensity conflict means that thousands of people die but slower than if you dropped a bomb on them in one fell swoop. It means that you infect the heart of the country, that you establish a malignant growth and watch the gangrene bloom. When the populace has been subdued — or beaten to death — the same thing — and your own friends, the military and the great corporations, sit comfortably in power, you go before the cameras and say democracy has prevailed. This was a commonplace in US foreign policy …"

POLITICAL PEACE

Over the centuries, a number of nations and tribes have developed a historical animosity and have been killing each other's children and grandchildren. In the 20th - century, a number of leaders have brought to the attention of their followers that they can continue their wars and lose more lives or make peace and end the cycle of violence.

I will quote two examples where two sets of political leaders, who were each other's enemies for years, even decades, rose above their animosity to break the cycle of violence and shook hands to create peace. One example was more successful than the other.

The first example was when Yitzak Rabin, the Israeli leader, shook hands with Yasser Arafat, the Palestinian leader. Both of them received the Nobel Peace Prize in 1994 admiring their efforts to create peace in the Middle East. It is interesting to note that both leaders were involved in an armed struggle before they embraced peace.

In his Nobel Lecture, Yasser Arafat stated, "We started the peace process on the basis of land for peace, and the basis of UN resolution 242 and 338, as well as other international decisions on achieving the legitimate rights of the Palestinian people." The same day Yitzak Rabin, in his Nobel Lecture thanked Yasser Arafat and his followers "who have chosen the path of peace and are writing a new page in the annals of the Middle East". It is sad that before Rabin and Arafat could bring their peace pregnancy full term, they experienced a political miscarriage because one fundamentalist, militant, extremist Jew assassinated Rabin, because in his view he did not want to see his leader shaking hands with the enemy. Rabin had to pay a heavy price for peace.

While Rabin and Arafat experienced a political miscarriage Mandela and de Klerk had a full-term political pregnancy and delivered democratic elections in South Africa and received Nobel peace Prizes. In their Nobel Lectures, both shared their peace philosophy. Mandela shared his vision of new South Africa and a new peaceful world in these words.

"We live with hope that as she battles to remake herself, South Africa will be like a microcosm of the new world that is striving to be born. This must be a world of democracy and respect for human rights, a world freed from the horrors of poverty, hunger, deprivation and ignorance, relieved of the threat and the scourge of civil wars and external aggression and unburdened of the great tragedy of millions forced to become refugees."

Mandela's partner in peace de Klerk in his Nobel lecture shared that, "There can be no real peace without justice and consent." He stated that peace is a frame of mind as well as a framework. He stated,

"Peace is a frame of mind".

It is a frame of mind in which countries, communities, arties and individuals seek to resolve their differences through agreements, through negotiation and compromise, instead of threats, compulsion and violence.

Peace is also a framework.

It is a framework within which the irresistible and dynamic processes of the social, economic and political development can be regulated and accommodated."

The more political leaders and their followers all over the world develop peace consciousness, the more they will find ways to overcome violent consciousness and to create a peaceful world. Economic, social and political peace, are just some of the colors of the peace rainbow that peaceful human beings are creating with their efforts.

Dear Kamran,

Let me finish this peace project with two of my poems, the first poem I had shared in the beginning of this project. I am sharing it again to complete the cycle for our readers. The second poem I want to share to highlight my perception of our special relationship and also the relationship with our readers. Such a relationship reflects that special connection that we need to work hard on, to create a peaceful world together. It is a dream but we need to dream before our peace dream becomes a reality.

Peacefully yours,

Sohail

~*~

PEACE

There is inner peace and there is outer peace
There is emotional peace and there is social peace
There is religious peace and there is political peace
There is local peace and there is global peace
These are all colors of peace
And we need all these colors
To create a rainbow of peace.

~*~

A VERY SPECIAL CONNECTION

You and I

Have a connection

A special connection

A very special connection

It is not a sexual, romantic or physical connection

It is rather an emotional, spiritual and creative connection

Such a connection

Cannot be defined

It transcends all definitions

It brings out the best in both of us

As two human beings

We are not only connected to each other

We are also connected to other human beings

With the passage of time

More and more people are becoming aware

Each human being is connected to the whole of humanity

The way

Each tree is connected to the jungle

Each flower is connected to the garden

Each star is connected to the galaxy

And

Each drop is connected to the ocean

It is an intimate connection

Two Candles of Peace

A loving connection

A magical connection

A mystical connection

A sacred connection

A human connection

One day we will realize

We are all

Part of the same family

The human family

The family of the heart.

~*~

Reviews of the Book

This is an incredible dialogue between two intellectuals with a common background in psychology, peace and philosophy, and the common goal of peace. The depth of knowledge, especially mastering the complex domains of spirituality, philosophy and mythology, is remarkable. Thoughts from Confucius to Joseph Campbell are not only mentioned but compared and analyzed with clarity and honesty. Even Buddha, the pinnacle of peace, gets his share of criticism. In addition to the advocate of peace, this dialogue would benefit anyone interested in the evolution of thought, spirituality and religion throughout the ages and across the globe. Such a synthesis is possible only after a lifetime of wide reading, immense reflection and a highly developed conscience. The politeness, civility and respect each offers the other are indicative of their deep sensitivity which drives their quest for peace. Whether offering their own insights — "Anything that moves the heart threatens them…" — to famous quotes — "Everything that lives is holy" — this dialogue is full of wisdom.

No single mortal can get everything right and so the two disagree at times. But here we see the highest standard of civility, as one writer points out a flaw in the other's view but accepts his own limitations and the other's advice with grace and humility. The reader may not agree with all that is offered, but will certainly be amazed at the depth of knowledge that generates these opinions and the breadth of subjects covered.

This dialogue certainly has resonance with today's issues of conflict and peace. It will also serve as an interesting insight, years hence, into what intellectuals of the early 21st century read their analyses and their conclusions. This dialogue will be read and discussed for many years on into the future.

Asif Niazi
Author of *Islam in the 21st Century*

~ * ~

In the book, *Two Candles of Peace*, the synergy of respect, reverence and love, that has been built between the authors, Dr. K Sohail and Dr. Kamran Ahmad, can be seen as boundless through their letters to each other, as they share their passion for peace, spirituality, psychology, and philosophy in their respective personal lives and careers. Each author, still so willing to give back to the individuals and to the world, their honesty and their help.

They light the written way, for the world to read their depth of international experience and knowledge on each page, as each exchanges words of wisdom. Words that weave throughout the hauntings of humanity and human rights; with heart-driven, heart-felt, humility and humbleness, yet peace of mind, peace of heart and peace of spirit always being the very strongest of threads in their individual and global quests.

It is an honour and a privilege to get to know these two authors on these pages. As the two people represent the two candles of peace that are willing to penetrate into the heart of darkness, religious extremism and political violence, to be willing to find on the other side, kindness, love and light within themselves, each other and those that become a part of their magical lives.

Laura Kay Snoddon
Poet and Writer

~ * ~

It's a fascinating read. The medium of e-mail dialogue chosen by the two authors adds to the casual and unencumbered flow. Through the easy-paced exchange the two authors enlighten the readers as they slide through struggles for internal peace in their world that includes living in multiple societies. The issues are magnified when the forces making for conflicts and the constant shaping and reshaping of values at the international level touch the personal level. The personal experiences are highlighted poignantly. Knotty topics in family life, love, sex, homosexuality, sectarianism, nationalism, mysticism, religion, spiritualism and activism, appear surreptitiously as the authors weave their individual personal lives in an unfinished and continuing search. The reader is constantly invited for reflection and will feel well-rewarded for the effort.

Abrar Hasan, Ph.D.

(Retired Head, Education Policy Division, OECD, Paris)

~ * ~

This is a rich and colorful combination of so many great writings, thoughts, and expertise. In these letters, two intellectuals have put up their experiences and reflections in an open and honest dialogue. The topics are diverse but have a flow of one idea to the other. Every letter creates a curiosity in the reader's mind to the next.

There are some potentially controversial topics on religion, human nature, socialism, and humanism that are not always easy to discuss. But the letters touch on them with such diligence, logic and softness that any reader would want to follow the dialogue and make sense of the logic.

At times a concept is explored so technically and with such detail, that as a reader you may find yourself a bit lost. But to receive the true essence of the subject, you must approach it actively and with curiosity, and then you will find each letter leading you to the next for answers. These letters are also a great source of information on important personalities, writers, philosophers, and spiritual gurus, where you appreciate the context and feel the interconnectedness of their work.

I have known Dr. Khalid Sohail for a few years now. Knowing Dr. Sohail, I feel, as Dr. Kamran feels, "I have stumbled upon a real-life Sufi." I become increasingly impressed by his wisdom, knowledge, humility, and inclusivity. A man with deep knowledge and humility, I would ascribe the following *shayr* [couplet] to Dr. Sohail:

Jo Alaa zarf hotay hain, hamesha jhuk ke miltay hain,

Surahi sar-nigoon ho kar bharra karti hay pemana

I have known Dr. Kamran more briefly and have only recently become acquainted with his works. But in our short interaction he came across as a soft, sensitive and down to earth person. His work on Sufism, spirituality, religion and psychology is impressive, especially his practical work for peace and humanity in the civil society of Pakistan. His letters reflect the diversity in his personality.

This book will be of great interest and benefit to those who are on any spiritual quest in their lives. This is certainly the case for me, as I was born and raised in a conservative environment in Peshawar, Pakistan but spent my adult life pursuing my career in the multicultural and multifaceted society of Canada. One can only imagine the questioning and reasoning of religious and cultural rituals, the efforts to explain and justify, only to be left feeling exhausted and confused. In a quest to find sense and purpose in religion, I find myself on the path to Sufism, and yet questioning ever more. The spiritual journey is one of question and answer and that is embodied in these letters. The letters will put such seekers both at ease on their path and take them deeper into the quest for clarity.

Dr. Khalida Nasim

www.ingramcontent.com/pod-product-compliance
Lightning Source LLC
Chambersburg PA
CBHW031508270326

41930CB00006B/302